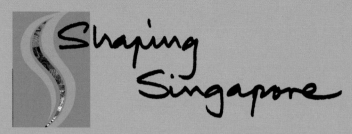

Shaping Singapore

a pictorial journey

through the lenses of 19 Singapore photojournalists

Achievements (1974-2004) & Aspirations (2004-2034)

Shaping Singapore

a pictorial journey

through the lenses of 19 Singapore photojournalists

Contents

We built this city

TODAY, Singapore's founding generation has time to smell the jasmine blossoms and step out in unison at line-dancing jamborees. Not so, less than 40 years ago, when having just gained Independence in 1965, simple survival was their consuming concern.

To think this modern city was built in just a couple of generations. Back then, not even the most optimistic of Singaporeans could have envisioned such a breathtaking city skyline, when the very sites of these skyscrapers were occupied by rundown urban slums.

Winning formula

Still, chance had little to do with the miracle of Singapore's physical transformation. Visionary planning was backed by bold political leadership and implemented through enlightened public-private sector collaboration. This is the winning formula that made possible the remarkable urban transformation which mirrors Singapore's economic blossoming.

As Singapore's planning authority, the story of the Urban Redevelopment Authority (URA) is closely tied with that of the Singapore miracle. Founded 30 years ago in April 1974, the URA continues to play a central role in guiding Singapore's physical development, both directly, and in a custodial manner in close collaboration with partner agencies.

Photojournalistic guide

To see Singapore's achievements in planning and urban design over the last 30 years, you only need look around you. Between these covers, you will see this reality through the lenses of 19 photojournalists who were asked to record the Singapore of 2004. They come from five national English, Chinese and Malay-language newspapers belonging to the Singapore Press Holdings stable – The Straits Times, Lianhe Zaobao, The New Paper, Berita Harian and Streats.

These images were exhibited in an exhibition entitled "**Shaping Singapore – Achievements (1974 - 2004) and Aspirations (2004 - 2034)**" held at The URA Centre from December 2004 to March 2005, of which this volume is the catalogue. As the title suggests, the exhibition also offers a glimpse of the exciting opportunities for the good life, business and fun in the Singapore of the next 30 years. This vision is included in the accompanying CD-Rom to this volume.

It is hoped that these images will anchor our memories of life in Singapore in 2004 and serve as a milestone to gauge our progress in collectively building the home of our dreams.

Reaping rewards – A member of Singapore's founding generation enjoying the fruit of her generation's labour at a line-dancing jamboree in the Padang

Photograph by *Spencer Chung Kun Soon*
Lianhe Zaobao

City of distinction

S INGAPORE is special. A tiny, resourceless dot on the face of the earth, Singapore has, nevertheless, been shaped into a city of superlatives.

Starting out as a remote 19th century colonial outpost, Singapore is, today, the best city in the world to visit. Singapore is also the safest city in the world. It is the home of Singapore Airlines, the best business airline in the world, which flies out of Changi Airport, which is, yes, the best airport in the world. The best business and leisure hotels in Asia – Shangri-la Hotel and Raffles Hotel, respectively – are also here.

Perennial perspective - Classic view of Singapore's skyline from the Singapore River

Photograph by *Lim Chye Leong*
URA

These accolades come, not from Singaporeans, but from Singapore's visitors. They are the 2004 findings of the British edition of Conde Nast Traveller magazine, regarded as the worldwide benchmark for the travel industry.

Larger than life
On the business front, Singapore is ranked No 1 among countries with populations under 20 million in international trade, labour market and basic and technological infrastructure (IMD World Competitiveness survey, 2003).

Hence, with a population of just 4.19 million and a land area of 697 square kilometres, Singapore's presence on the world stage is, quite literally, larger than life.

City of light – August fireworks thunder above Marina Bay

Photograph by *Dennis Thong Kah Hoong*
Lianhe Zaobao

FOL

Photography is the mastery of light, and photojournalism is the mastery of truth – telling stories with pictures, rather than words."

- *Edwin Koo,*
Streats photographer

01

The makings of a great city

Memorable Singapore

WHAT is it that makes us call this city our home?

Aside from the fact that, as Singaporeans, this is the place where we were born, the answer has to do with the collective memories we have gained and kept alive through our everyday experiences of the spaces in the city where we live, work and play. And which we hope to make even better, as a gift to our future generations to enjoy and build upon.

Planning and you

Planning and design – on an urban and architectural scale – may sound distant and even esoteric. But every day, planning and design impact on our lives. Every day, our decisions – from deciding where to meet friends for a meal, to investing in the dwelling of our dreams – are influenced by decisions made by planners, urban designers and architects. Indeed, the lives and livelihoods of entire generations of Singaporeans continue to be influenced by crucial planning decisions made during the formative years of the modern city of Singapore. Decisions made today will likewise influence the lives of future generations of Singaporeans.

Memories are made of these – the waters of the Singapore River have reflected Singapore's fortunes since Singapore's founder, Stamford Raffles, landed here in 1819 (right)

Photograph by *Mohd Ishak*
The New Paper

Let's count the ways – Singapore means different things to different people

URA Resource Centre

Making the right decisions

Have we succeeded in making the right decisions? Well, you only have to look around you and, if you are old enough, to cast your mind back to the 1960s when Singapore was vastly different: a slum-ridden and congested proposition. Singapore could have languished, and likely perished too – a possibility that can't be discounted out of hand. But thankfully, the government of the then newly self-governing Singapore could see the dire end of that road. In the early 1960s, they invited foreign experts to evaluate Singapore's state and propose courses of action. And they had the will to expunge existing plans, like the 1958 Master Plan drawn up by the British, and take the tough decisions necessary to implement the new plans.

A new Singapore

Through the following decades, Singapore, as we now know it, developed along the lines of these new plans. The photographs in this Folio entitled "The makings of a great city" portray aspects of Singapore that both Singaporeans and visitors alike find memorable. For Singaporeans, these are reminders of home when we are away from Singapore. For non-Singaporeans, they are the hallmarks that define Singapore as a distinctive destination for work or play, and even for making this their new home.

City of the new millennium – Pedestrians throng the seafront promenade by Marina Bay near the Esplanade - Theatres on the Bay (right)

Photograph by *Dennis Thong Kah Hoong*
Lianhe Zaobao

City of contrasts – Quaint pubs and eateries in Boat Quay's conserved shophouses hold their own against the CBD's titans (below)

Photograph by *Simon Ker*
The New Paper

Signature skyline

ADMIT it – flying in to Changi Airport, how often have you been able to resist the urge of marvelling, with quiet pride, at Singapore's magnificent skyline from the air?

Flying in at sunset - That fuzzy, warm feeling of arriving home is hard to beat

Photograph by *Casey Seyu Tzyy Wei*
Lianhe Zaobao

With thoughts of tucking into your favourite local food already in mind, have you not happily thought each time you touch down at Changi: "I'm home"?

Imagine then what might go through the mind of a visitor to Singapore as he or she flies in and experiences the gleaming airport, the magnificent avenue of tropical trees along East Coast Parkway, and then, rising to the top of Benjamin Sheares Bridge, the shimmering spires of the Central Business District (CBD) skyscrapers that constitute Singapore's signature skyline.

Beyond beautiful

Paris boasts "the world's most beautiful avenue" in its Champs Elysees. A picture postcard of London would show the Houses of Parliament and Big Ben on the River Thames.

Beyond being the subject of pretty postcards, being imageable brings tangible economic and cultural benefits to a city. For instance, to be able to attract international talent and business, there is a need for Singapore to retain and leverage on its unique identity as a city. Singapore's signature skyline certainly helps to brand Singapore as an attractive, distinctive and vibrant cosmopolitan city.

Photograph by *Stephanie Yeow*
The Straits Times

The lights never go out in the CBD – across global time zones, business transactions continue unabated day in, day out

Photograph by *Dennis Thong Kah Hoong*
Lianhe Zaobao

Crowning achievement

Whether viewed from the Singapore River, the Padang, or out at sea, the skyscrapers of the CBD rising above the historic city, illustrate Singapore's vitality as a nation. But this signature skyline didn't sprout by chance.

Its foundations were laid in the 1970s when the URA demarcated the boundary of the "Golden Shoe", as Singapore's CBD is known. Today, Singapore's signature skyline is the crowning achievement of the successful collaboration between the URA and private and public sector stakeholders in fulfilling the URA's vision of a great city to live, work and play in.

You've arrived!

Passage to the Lion City - the wide, manicured, verdant drive to town from Changi Airport makes for a memorable experience for the most jaded of travellers (above and right)

Photographs by *Long Kwok Hong*
Lianhe Zaobao

Look back in wonder – Arriving at Changi Airport is a world-class experience

Photograph by *Long Kwok Hong*
Lianhe Zaobao

WHEN pop superstar Janet Jackson was asked in a June 2004 interview what she remembered of her first whirlwind concert tour here in 1995, she said: "Clean. It's so clean it looks like you could eat off the streets."

It is a flattering, but not surprising impression, even coming from the most jet-set of people. After all, right from your arrival in Singapore, driving down the East Coast Parkway (ECP) into the city from Changi Airport, you would have experienced this memorable sight.

The smooth ride, through wide expanses of spotless greenery, with fleeting glimpses of the shimmering sea and high-rise apartment blocks through the tracery of rain trees overhead – you almost feel as if you have arrived in an earthly paradise. Especially after coming through Changi Airport, repeatedly rated the world's best by the travel industry over the years.

Photograph by *Ashleigh Sim*
Streats

First glimpse – Rising up Benjamin Sheares Bridge, the first glimpse of the city awaits (above and right)

Paradise road

In truth, the idea of a "parkway" was borrowed. The "parkway" concept adopted for the ECP originated in the USA. According to the American Heritage Dictionary, a parkway is a "broad landscaped highway, often divided by a planted median strip" – just what you see at the ECP. Only, flowering shrubs and a canopy of tropical trees have been used to attain the appearance of an urban wood. And an excellent maintenance programme by National Parks Board (NParks) ensures that it keeps its charming looks.

The ECP was conceived in the Concept Plan 1971 in which it was proposed that Singapore's new airport be located in Changi. Swift access between the new airport and the city was the need that sowed the seed for a parkway that would offer a welcoming experience for travellers entering Singapore by air. And one that will leave a lingering memory for departing visitors, including pop superstars.

Photograph by *Casey Seyu Tzyy Wei*
Lianhe Zaobao

Arenas of history

V ENICE has its Piazza San Marco. Beijing has its Tiananmen Square. And Singapore has its Padang as its arena of history. The physical scales may differ, but each is a space that is the focal point of national urban ritual – be it political, social or spiritual in nature.

The Padang, planned during the Raffles era and later enlarged to its present size, has always been maintained as an open space; a place for pomp and pageantry. While there are other open spaces in the city like Fort Canning Park and Hong Lim Park, the Padang's pre-eminence as Singapore's premier open space is unchallenged.

A space for all seasons – The Padang, Singapore's premier parade ground, is also a popular venue for sports, line-dancing and rock concerts. You have a choice of backdrops – the soaring CBD (right) or the imposing Supreme Court Building (page 27)

Photographs by *Joyce Fang*
The Straits Times

Photograph by *Spencer Chung Kun Soon*
The Straits Times

Padang, through the ages

In colonial times, the Padang was the choice venue for promenading. Today, sweaty soccer players and line-dancers replace umbrella-totting European ladies in their Victorian finery, so incongruous with the local weather.

As Singapore's premier celebratory space, the Padang was the venue for the swearing-in of Singapore's first president, Mr Yusof Ishak, on 3 December, 1959. It is the alternate venue of Singapore's National Day Parade. And also a venue for rock concerts by the likes of Linkin Park and performances by Cirque du Soleil.

Tropical formality

While in Europe, such a space would have been paved, the Padang (meaning "field" in Malay) is covered with grass – an appropriate climatic response that also allows it to function as a sporting arena. It is the grand green "forecourt" to Singapore's landmark civic buildings – the Supreme Court and City Hall – and also one of the island's oldest sports clubs, the Singapore Cricket Club, established in 1852.

The URA's Central Area Structure Plan (Appendix 6), published in 1985, sets out to ensure that the harmonious development of the city incorporates the preservation of such important places of urban memory as the Padang. Through other supporting urban design plans, such as the Civic District Plan and the Night Lighting Plan, these spaces are enhanced, and linked to other civic spaces. In implementing these ideas, the URA and its development partners ensure that such vital aspects of what it means to be Singaporean is preserved.

Historic moment – Singapore's first president Yusof Ishak being sworn in at the Padang in 1959. The National Loyalty Week was simultaneously launched

Photograph courtesy of *Ministry of Information, Communications and the Arts (MICA) Collection and National Archives of Singapore (NAS)*

Arenas of commerce

BEFORE it was named Raffles Place in 1853, this urban space was known as Commercial Square, a name that unequivocally signalled its purpose from Day One, a purpose which it fulfils eminently to this day.

No 1 from Day 1

Created in the days of Stamford Raffles by draining and filling a swamp adjacent to Boat Quay, Singapore's first banks and premier retailers promptly set up shop there. The Chartered Bank (established here in 1859) and the Hongkong and Shanghai Bank (1877), for instance, retain their presence at Raffles Place to this day, albeit in more modern forms. But other establishments like the Mercantile Bank, Kelly & Walsh bookshop and the John Little department store have been replaced by buildings of equally eminent establishments today – United Overseas Bank, Singapore Land and Caltex, among others.

Robinsons is now an Orchard Road stalwart after its premises at Raffles Place was razed by fire in 1972. John Little, however, retains a scaled-down presence here in the design of the entrances to the underground Raffles Place MRT station, which itself was built on the site of the Mercantile Bank, the first bank to be built at Raffles Place in 1855.

Continuing legacy

Over the years, Raffles Place has remained Singapore's premier arena of commerce. After all, Raffles Place is framed by the three tallest skyscrapers in Singapore, each rising 280m and constituting Singapore's signature skyline.

This, of course, is not the calling of caprice. But of a conscious planning decision to promote Raffles Place in particular, and the CBD in general, to be Singapore's most important commercial and banking centre. Today, the success of that decision is spectacularly evident for all to see.

Looking up in awe – Few have been able to resist visually scaling the sheer glass, granite and stainless steel walls of Raffles Place, Singapore's premier arena of commerce

Photograph by *Terence Tan*
The Straits Times

Same place, different era – Raffles Place was known as Commercial Square until 1853. In this 1930s postcard, the John Little store can be seen on the right, next to the Chartered Bank building

Photograph courtesy of
Mr Koh Seow Chuan

Same bank, different building – The Hongkong and Shanghai Bank building (on the left of the Medical Hall, late 1890s) still stands at Battery Road, albeit in a different form

Photograph courtesy of *NAS*

Same square, different style – This was what Raffles Place looked like in the 1960s. The plaza, with its floral clock, formed the roof of an underground carpark

Photograph by *Mr Lai Chee Weng*
URA Resource Centre

World at your fingertips – The pulse of world business is palpable at today's Raffles Place (left)

Photograph by *Terence Tan*
The Straits Times

Meteoric rise – The towers of Raffles Place were built on swamp land reclaimed during the Raffles era and designated "Commercial Square"

Photograph by *Lim Chye Leong*
URA

Down by the riverside

G OING against the grain of "polite" urban design norms can sometimes yield interesting results. At Boat Quay, the spectacular contrast created by the juxtaposition of the two- and three-storey historic shophouses with the 280m-high skyscrapers just a street away, is a case in point.

Thanks to this contrast, Singapore has a uniquely spectacular urban image that links its history with cutting-edge modernity. The contrast makes for a dramatic backdrop to memorable al fresco dining experiences at Boat Quay.

Vision fulfilled

Motivated by the desire to retain the historic quayscape which is synonymous with the founding of Singapore itself, the URA began planning for the conservation of Boat Quay in the mid-1980s. By July 1991, the shophouses facing the historic quay and those back-to-back with them had been restored through multi-agency and public-private sector collaboration, resulting in this characteristic contrast with the CBD skyscrapers.

Today, the URA's vision for the conservation of the Singapore River and its environs, including the construction of a 6km-long, 15m-wide continuous promenade on both banks of the river, has been realised. This promenade links the hallmark al fresco dining experience of Boat Quay with that of Clarke Quay further upstream, and urbane riverside-living at Robertson Quay.

To think that, not so long ago, for more than a hundred years, this same river was a stinking open sewer – until 1977, when Mr Lee Kuan Yew, Singapore's first Prime Minister, challenged government agencies and the people of Singapore to clean up and reinstate the Singapore River as an historic, commercial and recreational asset for the city.

Hotspot – A fixture in tourist guidebooks on Singapore, Boat Quay is also a popular nightspot among Singaporeans and expatriate executives from the neighbouring CBD

Photograph by *Mohd Ishak*
The New Paper

Belly of the carp – That's how the Singapore River at Boat Quay has been described. Thanks to conservation, colonial buildings on the north bank and shophouses on the south bank remain just as Raffles planned it

Photograph by *Wang Hui Fen*
The Straits Times

The night is young – As dusk descends upon the city, Boat Quay's al fresco scene stirs (left)

Photograph by *Mohd Ishak*
The New Paper

Things that go bump – Bumboats huddle together at a landing point in Clarke Quay. Building promenades, underpasses and boat landing points has made access to the Singapore River easier for pedestrians

Photograph by *Mohd Ishak*
The New Paper

24/7 metropolis

A TRULY metropolitan city is one where there's activity "24/7", or at all hours of the day and night, every day of the week. Already a city where you can walk alone at night without fear, Singapore has taken steps to become a quintessential metropolis that does not sleep.

In such a city, shopping and entertainment outlets remain open for longer hours. Today, places like Orchard Road, Albert Mall, China Square and Mohamad Sultan Road remain abuzz late into the night and, in some places, until the wee hours of the morning. This trend mirrors the 24-hour, globally-connected work cycle of the 21st century.

Bugis, Bugis burning bright

In June 1997, the URA unveiled its exciting plans for a bright and vibrant hub of entertainment activities focused in the Bugis area at the URA's E-Walk Exhibition. That subsequently set the stage for an arts and education hub that is being created here.

The URA then rolled up its sleeves and designed and built the 700 m long Albert Mall, one of the longest pedestrian malls in Singapore. The project was completed in May 1998. Today, the vibrant street life at Albert Mall attests to the success of this project, which sought to revitalise the area and make it a focal point for the local community and commercial activities.

Revellers' rave – Capitalising on its seafront location, al fresco dining near Merlion Park has taken off. Imagine this success replicated all around Marina Bay and you get the idea of Singapore of the future, a 24/7 metropolis

Photograph by *Dennis Thong Kah Hoong*
Lianhe Zaobao

Playing footsie – On 4m tall poles, to the thunderous beat of drums, lion dancers thrill with nail-biting acrobatics in a contest in Ngee Ann City (above)

Photograph by *Dennis Thong Kah Hoong*
Lianhe Zaobao

Meanwhile, at Orchard Road, the URA relaxed guidelines to encourage the setting up of outdoor refreshment areas in Singapore's premier hotel, tourist and shopping belt in July 1996. This added buzz at the outdoor, street-level to the already lively Orchard Road experience.

In May this year, the URA made available for sale the Urban Entertainment Centre project in the Bras Basah.Bugis area under the Reserve List system. This project is aimed at distinguishing this area as a vibrant city campus cum arts and entertainment zone, leveraging on its proximity to the newly established campuses of educational institutions like the LaSalle-SIA College of the Arts, Nanyang Academy of Fine Arts, and the Singapore Management University.

More "city-zens" to come

In addition to the bright prospects brought on by these developments, a larger resident population in the city will also anchor downtown vibrancy after office hours. The city's resident population is set to enjoy a boost when very high-rise, high-density residential projects such as the 46-storey Icon housing development, the 50-storey The Pinnacle@Duxton public housing scheme, and The Sail, a 70-storey residential development in the Downtown at Marina Bay are completed.

Streetside treat – People-watching on busy Orchard Road over a cuppa (left)

Photograph by *Yap Lay Bee*
URA

Sleepless in Singapore – At a glance, you'd be forgiven thinking this is Manhattan. Standing spectacularly at 280m high, Singapore's three tallest skyscrapers puncture the horizon, as the streets below glow golden with the evening CBD traffic (right)

Photograph by *Dennis Thong Kah Hoong*
Lianhe Zaobao

Colour me beautiful – Nightfall brings even more colour to the streetlife of Little India as street markets come to life

Photograph by *Casey Seyu Tzyy Wei*
Lianhe Zaobao

Eat under the stars – Lanterns and neon lights herald an evening's gastronomic adventures on "food street", Chinatown

Photograph by *Spencer Chung Kun Soon*
Lianhe Zaobao

Candy-coloured city – It's worth the trip just to take in the lights of Orchard Road. Shopping centres vying to be best and brightest add buzz to Singapore's premier shopping street

Photograph by *Spencer Chung Kun Soon*
Lianhe Zaobao

Arts and the city

G LOBAL cities share a common trait in their metropolitan make-up. Mention London, New York and Sydney, and, aside from their physical distinctiveness as cities, their vibrant cultural life comes to mind. These cities are magnets for top performers and orchestras, as well as exhibitions of the visual arts, which in turn, attract people from all over the world who may travel to the prestigious venues in these cities just to catch a show.

Symbiotic relationship

The arts and cities have enjoyed a symbiotic relationship throughout history. City fathers traditionally build grand performance venues which, in turn, are the symbols of the cultural pride of those cities. And so the Sydney Opera House is instantly recognisable as the "international dhoby mark" of Sydney. Just as the Guggenheim Museum Bilbao is synonymous with the Basque city.

Likewise, the Esplanade - Theatres on the Bay, referred to affectionately by locals as "The Durian" after the strong-smelling "king of fruits" native to these parts, has begun to assume an iconic mantle for Singapore. Its unusual spiky fenestration, bulbous form and prominent position on the city seafront opposite the other symbol of Singapore – the Merlion – has put it on postage stamps, postcards and coffee table books on Singapore, as well as the programme sheets of world-class music, theatre and dance performances.

Rose among the stones – Enjoying the "company" of renowned Taiwanese sculptor Ju Ming's sharp-suited executives at The Fullerton Hotel

Photograph by *Long Kwok Hong*
Lianhe Zaobao

Talk to me – Students checking out life before their time, as depicted in "Great Emporium" by Malcolm Koh (above)

Photograph by *Simon Ker*
The New Paper

Making our mark

In alignment with Singapore's "City in a Garden" image and to promote the appreciation of public urban art indoors as well as in parks and plazas, the URA launched the Public Sculptures Master Plan in September 2002.

At the same time, the URA identified a site, designed and implemented the new Merlion Park fronting Marina Bay in collaboration with the Singapore Tourism Board (STB). The Merlion sculpture, Singapore's tourist icon, was moved to where it is visible from Marina Bay, around which Singapore's exciting Downtown at Marina Bay will be built, set against Singapore's signature skyline.

Pastime from the past – Before there was bungee-jumping, youthful thrill-seekers sought the adrenaline rush from jumping into rivers and ponds. "First Generation" at Boat Quay is by Chong Fah Cheong (left)

Photograph by *Long Kwok Hong*
Lianhe Zaobao

Blossoming BBB

The foundation has already been laid for the spectacular flowering of arts, culture, learning and entertainment activities at the Bras Basah.Bugis area in the next two years, following its identification and designation in 1996 by the URA for such activities. Through close liaison with Ministry of Information, Communications and the Arts (MICA) and Ministry of Education (MOE), numerous arts groups and arts education campuses have sunk roots in the area. These include the Young Musicians' Society, Action Theatre, Dance Ensemble Singapore and the new campus of the Nanyang Academy of Fine Arts, which has recently opened.

The eagerly anticipated opening of the new National Library and the campuses of the LaSalle-SIA College of the Arts and the Singapore Management University (SMU) will soon follow. The influx of artists, and some 16,000 students from the new educational institutions, will be a major shot in the arm for the artistic and commercial life of the district. The incorporation of some of SMU's public facilities within Bras Basah Park, framing the vista between the historic Singapore Art Museum and the Singapore History Museum will see it reinvigorated as a focal point for student and public activities in the heart of the Civic District.

Newest icon

Arguably, the single biggest event in the Singapore arts scene was the spectacular opening of the Esplanade - Theatres on the Bay on 12 October, 2002. As much as being the newest Singapore icon, its world-class performance facilities have attracted world-class acts here.

Larger than life – One of Roy Lichtenstein's "Six Brushstrokes", 1996 series, at Millenia Singapore

Photograph by *Ho Peng Yew*
Lianhe Zaobao

Drama zone – Bras Basah.Bugis is a hotbed of the arts, with numerous arts groups like Action Theatre sinking roots there

Photograph by *Wee Su Lin*
URA

Art zone – The Community Art Project is just one of many art-related activities that have brightened the streetscape of the Bras Basah.Bugis area

Photograph by *Yeo Pei San*
URA

Durians are best – Many Singaporeans believe so, both about the king of fruits, and The Esplanade

Photograph by *Long Kwok Hong*
Lianhe Zaobao

Fly-eye's view – The city skyline through The Esplanade's spiky fenestration for which it has been variously dubbed "durian", "microphone", and "fly's eyes" (right)

Photograph by *Long Kwok Hong*
Lianhe Zaobao

Between the sea and a spiky place – The Merlion (left) is Singapore's most iconic emblem after Singlish, local food and the national flag, according to a National University of Singapore Political Students Association poll of 750 undergraduates in September 2004

Photograph by *Lee Tiah Khee*
Lianhe Zaobao

This way to culture – In its first year of operations, 6.1 million people visited The Esplanade. It has held 1,489 performances by 18,986 artists, sold 356,742 tickets and hosted 555,467 people to free performances (right)

Photograph by *Long Kwok Hong*
Lianhe Zaobao

FOL

Photography intercepts reality as it exists.

*- **John Berger**,*
art critic for The Observer newspaper

02

Planning a nation's needs

In the beginning

THE Singapore of 30 years ago was not this clean, efficient, and pleasant place you see today. Despite Lt Jackson's 1822 plan (Appendix 1) that demarcated neat ethnic enclaves, the city had become chronically congested as migrants kept arriving, attracted by Singapore's prosperity as a free port sitting astride the lucrative East-West shipping route.

Planning vacuum
The squalor of squatters was the consequence of over 100 years of unbridled urban development until the Singapore Improvement Trust was set up to address Singapore's urban problems in 1927. Planners refer to this period as the "planning vacuum".

Even the opening up of the island's interior, with the laying of Bukit Timah and Thomson Roads in the 1890s, didn't relieve the pressures of over-population, which had breached the 1 million mark by 1947.

By the time Singapore achieved self-government in 1959, it had already risen to become a regional commercial hub. But Singapore's unemployment and a severe housing crunch were her two most pressing problems.

Birth of modern Singapore
It was not until the late 1960s and 1970s that things began to change. The hallmarks of

One nation, many needs - Despite scarce resources, Singapore's planners have to ensure sufficient land for business, port activities, housing, recreation, greenery, and industry - as this panorama from Sentosa Island illustrates

Photograph by *Ng Chor Seng*
URA

modern Singapore took root, in particular, with her innovative public housing scheme, garden city image, and forward-looking physical planning that was systematically executable. These developments were marked by the formation of the Planning Department and Housing Development Board (HDB) in 1960.

Within the HDB, an Urban Renewal Department (URD) was formed in 1966, and in April 1974, the URA was born to facilitate the increasingly important role that physical planning and urban design played in the creation of Singapore's Central Area. By then, the planners had published the Concept Plan 1971 (Appendix 5), Singapore's first long-range development plan.

The process of creating modern Singapore, as we know it today, had begun in earnest.

Public living room – As recently as 50 years ago, chronic congestion in Singapore's inner city meant that much of life was enacted in the five-footways

Photograph courtesy of *K F Wong Collection and NAS*

Foreign designs

PRIOR to Singapore's Independence in 1965, its planning was left largely to foreigners - primarily, the British, Singapore's colonial masters since Raffles' days. After self-rule in 1959, United Nations planners were invited by the Singapore government in 1962 and 1963 to help chart new planning directions for the island's future.

Classic colony

The colonial mindset of the British was demonstrated in Lt Jackson's plan of 1822 (Appendix 1) in which the different ethnic groups were accorded separate enclaves. The European Town occupied the prime area on the Singapore River's north bank, while the Chinese were settled on the south bank. The Chuliahs, Arabs and Bugis had areas beyond the European Town. Today, the basic road structure of the city and Raffles Place as "Commercial Square" remain as a legacy of Lt Jackson's plan.

But for more than 100 years afterwards, growth continued without any long-range vision. Urban amenities were overburdened with 25 per cent of the population squeezed into 1 per cent of Singapore's total land area. With as many as 100 people living in one shophouse, the slums were both a health and fire hazard, as evident in a fire that swept the Bukit Ho Swee area in 1961, leaving 16,000 people homeless.

Though the Singapore Improvement Trust was set up by the colonial government in 1927, its efforts were too piecemeal to make any impact on Singapore's burgeoning urban problem. Queenstown and Toa Payoh were designated as New Towns during this period to alleviate the overcrowding in the city.

The morning after – Aerial view of the city circa 1965 shows a congested city on the brink of redevelopment

Photograph courtesy of *NAS*

Structure retained – Raffles' legacy to the city remains in its basic arterial road structure. This is reinforced with the designation of conservation areas such as Chinatown, which developed on lands designated to the various Chinese dialect communities by Raffles

Photograph by *Spencer Chung Kun Soon*
Lianhe Zaobao

In 1958, Singapore's first statutory Master Plan (Appendix 2) was published.

Wiping the slate clean

Within four years, however, the 1958 Master Plan was declared obsolete by Professor Erik Lorange, a Norwegian architect-planner who led the first UN planning team invited here in 1962 by the newly self-governing Singapore. The 1958 plan was criticized as being too conservative in maintaining the Euro-centric status quo. Instead, Lorange proposed an action-oriented "precinctal" plan (Appendix 3), two precincts of which - at Crawford Road and Outram Road - were completed by the government.

The following year, another UN team led by Professor Otto Koenigsberger, a German architect-planner, arrived to propose a "ring city" plan (Appendix 4) for a future population of 4 million and incorporating a mass rail transport system. This plan, based on the Dutch model where a ring of towns encircle and is supported by a central hinterland, laid the foundation for the strategic focus of Singapore's planning.

Singaporeans at the helm

WITH self-rule in 1959 and Independence in 1965, planning Singapore's future became the responsibility of Singaporeans.

First long-range plan

Following the United Nations planners' visits to Singapore in 1962 and 1963, a task force called the State and City Project team (SCP) was formed, comprising members from the Planning Department, HDB (including URD) and the Traffic Unit of the Public Works Department. Between 1967 and 1971, the SCP team worked on the recommendations of the UN planners, producing Singapore's Concept Plan 1971, which was Singapore's first long-range plan.

Concept Plan 1971 (Appendix 5) proposed a transport framework, new satellite towns, industrial zones and a central commercial centre to promote industrialisation and economic growth. This plan was used by the Planning Department to guide the physical development of Singapore.

The URA was created in April 1974 to focus on the increasingly important role that physical planning and urban design played in the redevelopment of Singapore's Central Area.

Land sales - a key tool

To enable redevelopment to take place, the URD and its successor, the URA, was empowered to clear slums and sell assembled plots of land upon which the nexus of Singapore's economic growth would be built.

This was implemented through the Government Land Sales (GLS) programme. As the government's lead land sales agency, the URA was instrumental in these early years in enabling the transformation of the slum-filled city centre to the modern financial and business hub it is today.

In 1985, to guide the shaping of the skyline and create a city that harmoniously interweaves its modern buildings with its historic fabric, the URA drew up the Central Area Structure Plan (Appendix 6).

Leavin' on a jetplane – Changi Airport is the best airport in the world according to international surveys by influential travel magazines Conde Nast Traveller (UK), Travel Savvy, and Business Traveller (Asia Pacific) which voted it No 1 for 13 straight years. Changi Airport was first mooted in the Concept Plan 1971

Photograph by *Tukiman Warji*
Berita Harian

Concept Plan 1991 (Appendix 7)

The vision was to create a tropical city of excellence while sustaining economic growth and providing a good quality of life. The key thrusts of the 1991 Plan that have been achieved are the:

- Provision of a wider variety of housing types
- Creation of new parks and park connectors while improving established parks
- Development of regional centres at Tampines, Jurong East and Woodlands
- Reclamation of Jurong Island as a petro-chemical hub
- Expansion of the MRT and LRT network
- Development of the Technology Corridor by opening the Changi and International Business Parks
- Development of a vibrant arts and culture scene.

Concept Plan 2001 (Appendix 8)

The Concept Plan 2001 aims to make Singapore a thriving world-class city in the 21st century. The key strategies of the Plan which are now being implemented are:

- New homes in familiar places
- High-rise city living
- More choices for recreation
- Greater flexibility for businesses
- Global business centre
- Extensive rail network
- Focus on identity

In March 1989, the URA extended its planning and conservation jurisdiction island-wide when the Planning Department and Research & Statistics Unit of the Ministry of National Development came under its roof.

Concept Plan series

To facilitate sustained economic growth, a good quality of life, and to make Singapore a tropical city of excellence, the URA published the Concept Plan 1991, based on decentralisation of development for a long-term projected population of 4 million.

In April 2001, the URA entered a new phase with a new mission statement: "To make Singapore a great city to live, work and play". In July 2001, the URA revealed how it will achieve this mission through the Concept Plan 2001, which will guide Singapore's physical development for the next 40 to 50 years. This plan incorporated the feedback from 10 months of extensive public consultation.

The Master Plan 1998, which comprehensively spelt out the planning intentions for every plot of land in Singapore, was published in January 1999. This has since been updated as the Master Plan 2003.

Building on past efforts – Housing at Tanjong Rhu (foreground), builds on the success of the Government Land Sales programme, whose first sale in 1967 was of three commercial sites in the Golden Mile across Kallang River (above)

Photograph by *Casey Seyu Tzyy Wen, Lianhe Zaobao*

Decentralising development – Three Regional Centres
- in Tampines, Woodlands and Jurong East - were proposed in
Concept Plan 1991. Residents in Jurong East (below) will have the
option to work in their neighbourhood

Photograph by *Dennis Thong Kah Hoong*
Lianhe Zaobao

Of highways and reclamations

I N tandem with efforts to clear up slums in the city centre for commercial developments on larger plots of land, the downtown area was also enlarged through reclamation.

By the 1970s, the reclamation of 690 hectares of land southeast of the city centre had been planned, to form Marina Centre, South and East for the future expansion of the city. This is a dream come true for city planners, presenting a unique opportunity to create a new city unhampered by outmoded infrastructure, roads or buildings.

Marina East, Centre and South

Marina Centre was planned as an extension of the Orchard Road hotel and shopping belt. The first sale of site here - Marina Square, an integrated hotel, convention and shopping hub - was completed in 1978.

Marina South, being adjacent to the existing CBD, presented prime prospects for the extension of the business and financial hub at Shenton Way and Raffles Place. Marina South originated as a mere spit of land upon which the East Coast Parkway-Benjamin Sheares Bridge lay, following the planning decision that it would run over the sea and not through the city centre. With the spit of land thus almost enclosing an area of the sea, the reclamation of Marina South followed its outline.

Marina East is the largest of the three reclaimed tracts. It is largely a reserve site which is being studied for residential and recreational uses.

Say cheese – From the top of Millenia Tower, through a 15mm fish-eye lens, the Benjamin Sheares Bridge is Singapore's urban smiley. The three tracts of reclaimed land are separated by the Kallang and Singapore River basins

Photograph by *Ho Peng Yew*
Lianhe Zaobao

Urban waterfront

Together, the three tracts of reclaimed land define Marina Bay and Kallang Basin, covering 284 hectares of water and promising ample opportunities for water sports and recreation. Upon the completion of a barrage across the channel leading to Marina Bay and Kallang Basin in mid-2007, an urban reservoir will be formed.

Downtown at Marina Bay

In the mid-1980s, the URA focused on the development of a new downtown for the 21st century on reclaimed land around Marina Bay. This concept was expanded to offer an integrated live-work-play environment on the 360 hectares of reclaimed land, and was unveiled in August 1996 as "A City of the Future".

To catalyse investment for developments at Marina Bay, the URA commenced building the Common Services Tunnel network here to house integrated utilities in underground tunnels in May 2001. Two sites here have also been sold in 2001 and 2002, and the NTUC Headquarters completed in 2004.

This year sees further developments for the realisation of the Downtown at Marina Bay. In April 2004, the invitation for tender for an International Design Consultancy for the waterfront promenade and bridge at Downtown at Marina Bay was launched. And in May 2004, the Business Financial Centre site in Downtown at Marina Bay was made available for sale on the Reserve List of the Government Land Sales (GLS) Programme.

Landfall – Land reclamation, which created East Coast Park and part of the CBD in the distance, is as old as Singapore itself, with the first efforts commenced during Raffles' time to create Commercial Square next to Boat Quay

Photograph by *Ashleigh Sim*
Streats

Hop, skip, jump – Skirting the city, Benjamin Sheares Bridge came into existence with the planning decision to have trans-island traffic circumvent the city centre

Photograph by *Casey Seyu Tzyy Wei*
Lianhe Zaobao

Seas of gold – Cars and cruisers cross paths, bathed in glorious light

Photograph by *Casey Seyu Tzyy Wei*
Lianhe Zaobao

Key to development

From its beginnings in 1967, the Government Land Sales (GLS) Programme has been instrumental in implementing the development plans for Singapore. With the government owning more than 90 per cent of the land, the URA, as the government's key land sales agent, was able to combine land use planning with the GLS to create value from raw land and dilapidated properties, open up investment opportunities and channel private capital to Singapore's economic development.

Key development tool

Bringing plans to reality is an elaborate process that starts years ahead. In the 1960s, the URD cleared slums, rehoused displaced businesses, prepared guide plans and assembled lands for sale for unencumbered development. These efforts transformed the Golden Shoe into Singapore's modern CBD. Elsewhere, the GLS programme was instrumental in the development of Suntec City, Marina Centre, the Singapore River, China Square and Tanjong Rhu. About 1,400 sites, covering 840 hectares, have been sold through the GLS programme. This has generated 2 million square metres of office space, 1.3 million square metres of shops, 12,000 hotel rooms and 52,000 private housing units, making up between 25 and 40 per cent of the total island-wide stock.

Building landmarks

By collaborating with developers through the GLS, the URA has been able to ensure good architecture at prominent sites and facilitate Singapore's evolution into a city of excellence. Detailed urban design guidelines are incorporated into the sale so that developers are clear about these requirements from the onset. This collaboration has produced such notable landmarks as the OCBC Centre, Marina Square, OUB Centre, and Suntec City.

Sold! – This cluster of commercial landmarks is the result of the
URA's role as the Government's key land sales agent in carrying
out the GLS programme

Photograph by *Ho Peng Yew*
Lianhe Zaobao

Some GLS developments have won international awards. The developer of One Raffles Link and CityLink Mall, completed in 2000, bagged an Urban Land Institute - Award of Excellence 2002 (Small-scale, Mixed-use Development) for its superior planning, design and development.

In 2001, the developer of Far East Square, a mixed conservation-redevelopment project, won the FIABCI Prix d'Excellence (Specialised Category) award given out by the International Real Estate Federation for excellence in all real estate disciplines involved in the project's creation.

Greater flexibility

One of the key strengths of the Singapore land use planning system is the ability to implement plans through the GLS programme. However, in response to changing business needs, the URA has guided the evolution of the GLS programme to meet these needs. It has been used as a platform to introduce new development concepts like "white" sites (October 1995), the reserve list system (June 2001) and, recently, an option scheme for the sale of the Business and Financial Centre (BFC) site at the Downtown at Marina Bay. This will allow a master developer to develop the BFC in phases.

A "white" site gives developers the flexibility to decide on a range of commercial, hotel or residential uses. Under the reserve list system, sites will only put up for tender if the Government receives a commitment from developers to bid at an acceptable minimum price, enabling the GLS programme to be more responsive to market conditions.

Phoenix rising – Singapore's CBD was largely built on squatter or reclaimed land whose development potential was unlocked through URA's planning and urban design guidelines and facilitated through the GLS programme and private sector initiatives

Photograph by *Dennis Thong Kah Hoong*
Lianhe Zaobao

Making space

W ITH urban redevelopment set in motion, URA's urban designers concentrated on creating and improving the quality of spaces in the city.

At Orchard Road and Raffles Place, comprehensive pedestrian networks of covered walkways and underground malls are in various stages of completion.

Through its urban design guidelines, public spaces such as those at Ngee Ann City, Suntec City and Bugis Junction, and "city rooms" such as at UOB Plaza were created.

Working in collaboration with partners like the National Parks Board, parks like the Marina City Park were created in anticipation of the development of the Downtown at Marina Bay.

Sculptural presence

Plazas and promenades are graced with fountains and sculptures by world-famous artists like Salvador Dali ("Homage to Newton" at UOB Plaza), Henry Moore ("Reclining Figure" at OCBC Centre), Fernando Botero ("Bird" at Boat Quay), Roy Lichtenstein ("Six Brushstrokes" at Millenia Tower), Robert Indiana ("LOVE" at Penang Road) and Sun Yu Li (Celestial Earth at The URA Centre) among others.

Wet 'n' wild – Bugis Junction, an integrated office, retail and hotel development boasts Singapore's first air-conditioned shopping street. It won the Singapore Institute of Architects (SIA) Architectural Design Award for urban design in 1998. The interactive fountain is a hit with the children

Photograph by *Ho Peng Yew*
Lianhe Zaobao

Local lore has not been forgotten - sculptures that remind us of life in Singapore's pre-modern times by local artists can be found along the Singapore River and pocket parks like the one at Telok Ayer. In these places, works like Lee Leong Seng's "Chinese Processions" and Chong Fah Cheong's "First Generation - Boys Jump Into The River" transport the viewer to the life and times of a bygone era. They have now become part of the Singapore urban experience.

Plans such as the Civic District Lighting Plan & Guidebook, launched in June 1995 by the URA and the Singapore Tourism Board, have helped to ensure that these urban assets continue to build on Singapore's distinctiveness.

Photograph by *Spencer Chung Kun Soon*
Lianhe Zaobao

Fair game – From family board games to acrobatic antics, the plaza at Ngee Ann City has proven to be popular with pedestrians and event organisers alike. It was an urban design requirement as part of the development of Ngee Ann City (above and right)

"Birdie ngam ngam" – And poo poo here;
Botero's "Bird" at Boat Quay elicits an animated
response

Photograph by *Alan Lim*
The Straits Times

Photograph by *Dennis Thong Kah Hoong*
Lianhe Zaobao

Distinct districts

In 2003, the URA also produced the Public Space & Urban Waterfront Master Plan which seeks to highlight the unique strengths and natural attributes of the various districts in the city centre.

This plan proposes to enhance existing key activity areas such as Orchard Road, Singapore River, the CBD and Bugis by building a variety of public spaces and encouraging the provision of such spaces within selected private developments.

One of the boys – Giant advertising billboard presides over a street soccer game at Duxton Plain (right)

Photograph by *Low Chwee Lye*
URA

Lichtenstein's legacy – Roy Lichtenstein's "Six Brushstrokes", a set of free-standing sculptures stand in a plaza designed by the artist at Millenia Tower. It was one of his last works

Photograph by *Ho Peng Yew*
Lianhe Zaobao

Minding your business

POWER to the people – URA was the first government agency to include private sector participants in its POWER sessions

Photographs by *Ng Chor Seng*
URA

C OMMUNICATION is the key to taking a pro-business stance in implementing plans. Recognising this, the URA has taken the initiative to engage its partner agencies and stakeholders on all fronts of its activities to understand their business needs better. These outreach initiatives range from meetings with developers or building owners on sales sites and development applications, to collaborations with professional institutes on exhibitions and publications, to POWER sessions.

Cutting red tape
POWER (Public Officers Working to Eliminate Red-tape) was an initiative by the Ministry of Finance in January 2001 to cut red-tape. The URA felt that the POWER idea would benefit those affected by its Development Control (DC) rules. So the URA took the idea one step further by being the first to invite private sector users of its rules to participate. Since then, three POWER sessions have been held.

The first session, in January 2002 looked at guidelines for industrial development. The second, in August 2002, focused on flats and condominiums, at which architects, real estate developers and consultants, engineers, residents, journalists and representatives from the Feedback Unit participated.

Out of the 30 guidelines put up for review in these first two sessions, 23 recommendations were accepted, including some which argued for keeping the guidelines discussed. The third POWER session in 2003 reviewed guidelines for commercial, hotel and mixed use developments.

"White" sites
Being pro-business also means being flexible in achieving its planning objectives. To this end, the URA introduced the concept of "white" sites in October 1995 when it sold the first two sites at China Square and Middle Road. In "white" sites, developers are allowed to mix and vary residential, commercial and hotel uses within their developments without the need for land use rezoning. An example of a project built on a "white" site is the upcoming Soho@Central at Clarke Quay MRT station - and the recently completed NTUC Headquarters.

New kid on the block – Fireworks herald the completion of the first development on the Downtown at Marina Bay site - the NTUC HQ - a "white" site (right)

Photograph by *Ho Peng Yew*
Lianhe Zaobao

Your ideas count

M ORE and more, the public is being consulted on Singapore's long-term development plans.

In the past, feedback was sought only after draft plans were drawn and exhibited. The final plans would then incorporate your feedback. These days, the URA consults you even before the draft plans are drawn, so as to register your input at the earliest possible moment. The whole idea is that, if these plans are for the development of Singapore, then you should have a say in them.

Incorporating your ideas

The URA's first experience in public consultation for its development plans was in

1989 with the Civic District Plan, on which members of the architectural and related professions were consulted.

In 1992, the URA's consultative approach was applied to the drawing up of the 55 Development Guide Plans (DGPs) covering Singapore. With three stages to the drawing up of DGPs - collecting and analysing data, drafting and public exhibition to gather feedback - each DGP took an average of two years to complete. But the effort was worthwhile. The feedback received through extensive public dialogues improved these detailed local plans and clearly informed landowners and developers on what they can do with each piece of land.

The DGPs were completed in July 1998. Together, the DGPs constituted the Master

Turning the tide – The public's passionate pleas for Chek Jawa's retention gave the ecological gem a new lease of life in 2001

Photograph by *Stephanie Yeow*
The Straits Times

Plan 1998 that guided the physical development of Singapore in an open, transparent way.

Consulting you even earlier

The Concept Plan is a plan that guides the long-term development of Singapore. Revised every 10 years, the 2001 edition of the Concept Plan was unprecedented in that even before the draft was drawn, public feedback was already sought. This was done through e-consultation and two focus groups, which, over a period of four months, deliberated on planning dilemmas, and helped shape the draft plan. The draft plan was then exhibited for further feedback before it was finalised.

For implementation, the Concept Plan is translated into more detailed, shorter term Master Plans. As with its 1998 edition, the Master Plan 2003 was gazetted after extensive public consultation. This included the feedback gathered through the exhibition of the Parks and Waterbodies Plan and Identity Plan, five regional exhibitions of the Draft Master Plan, subject group discussions and stakeholder dialogues. In this way, the final version of Master Plan 2003 facilitates the attainment of a good quality of life, greater business flexibility and a stronger sense of identity in the built environment.

Double delight – Curiosity is written all over the faces of these urban boys encountering a hermit crab at Chek Jawa (above)

Protected species – Crowds descended on Chek Jawa to see, first-hand, what they feared would be lost forever (below)

Photographs by *Stephanie Yeow*
The Straits Times

Writing guidelines together

The URA also actively sought public feedback on the formation and review of policies that affect the public, such as the development of the Landscape Deck, a new alternative building form. The guidelines for this development type were drawn up in consultation with professional bodies and were posted for public e-consultation on URA's website for two months. E-consultation has also been conducted to ascertain childcare centre needs in landed housing estates.

e-xcellent service

WHILE the URA played its key national role as Singapore's planning and conservation authority, it has also maintained a keen focus on providing excellent public service.

With the advent of the Internet and widespread electronic access by its customers, the URA employed e-services to enhance its customers' convenience and efficiency.

Electronically yours
In March 1998, the URA launched the Electronic Development Application (EDA) system. This is a major boon to architectural practices - one of the URA's main customer groups - who can send their applications for building works for URA's approval at the click of a mouse, from the comfort of their home or office, at any time of day.

EDA also resulted in the processing time for development applications being halved from eight weeks to just four.

First born – Ulu Pandan Community Centre was the first public project that was submitted through EDA to be completed

Photograph by *Tukiman Warji*
Berita Harian

In March 2002, the EDA system was submitted to the Commonwealth Association for Public Administration and Management (CAPAM) International Innovations Awards Programme. This award is given out to recognise organisations that are truly innovative. The URA was awarded the Certificate of Achievement for being ranked among the top 30 of 150 submissions from countries world wide.

For the stakeholders in the real estate business, who require timely information on Singapore's property market, the URA launched the online subscription-based Real Estate Information System in November 2001.

Click "Send" for feedback
The general public is also an important URA customer. To ensure that feedback given by its public customers is managed consistently, the URA launched its Customer Information System (CIS) in 2004. The CIS provides URA with a consistent framework to profile, track and respond to our customers, and provides ease of routing to the relevant section for follow-up.

More importantly, to the public, the CIS allows for an improved response time since service standards, e-alerts, and reference to the history of the enquiry are built-in.

No more chasing the warden
One area where continuous improvements in service has been made since the 1980s has been in car park management. Before 1980, drivers actually had to look for a parking warden to pay for their parking under the Advice Note system, a tough task especially on rainy days. In February 1980, the URA put an end to that practice by introducing the self service Coupon Parking System.

How far we have come since. In 1992 drivers could renew URA season parking tickets via GIRO. In 1994, it was possible to do e-payment of parking fines, via Self-Service Automated Machines (SAM), telephone and Automated

Making it easier – With EDA, you can submit your plans from home, or from any of these dedicated public EDA terminals at The URA Centre

Photograph by *Lim Chye Leong*
URA

Teller Machines (ATM). From November 2001, this, and applying for season parking tickets, was also possible via the Internet.

In April 2002, URA's online parking services were further extended to include the transfer, replacement and renewal of season parking tickets, vehicle permit certificate application and payment, and appeal on parking fines. At the same time, online Lodgement Notification for Use of Temporary Vehicle was introduced so that motorists need not come to the URA office to apply for temporary parking labels when their vehicles are temporarily not in use.

FOL

"Photography, the mainstay of illustrative journalism, is an effective means of communication. A picture can tell a better story than a thousand words, and in a language that can be understood by people of different races."

- David Tay,
CEO, SPH Magazines Pte Ltd
President, Photographic Society of Singapore

03

Singapore River

Enduring lifeline

CITIES usually begin life at the confluence or mouth of a river, and Singapore is no exception. Even before Raffles landed 185 years ago, when Singapore was little more than a swampy isle, the mouth of the Singapore River already harboured a settlement of Orang Laut.

Everything we could desire

"This place possesses an excellent harbour and everything that can be desired for a British port....we have commanded an intercourse with all the ships passing through the Straits of Singapore. In short, Singapore is everything we could desire, and I may consider myself most fortunate in its selection; it will soon rise into importance."

These were Raffles' words after signing the agreement with the Temenggong on 30 January 1819 to secure British interests in Singapore. History has proven him correct: after Raffles established Singapore as a free port at the commercial crossroads of east-west maritime traffic, the Singapore River emerged as the nexus of the colony's trade, attracting three quarters of all shipping business by the 1860s.

Living links – Like these bumboats moored to the quay, Singapore's history is closely tied with that of the Singapore River, which has retained its relevance to contemporary Singapore life over the years

Photograph by *Mohd Ishak*
The New Paper

Victim of her own success

Despite dredgings, reclamations, and other expedient attempts at improving its capacity to contain the burgeoning traffic plying its waters, the Singapore River soon suffered from the massive congestion and gross pollution from overuse.

By the 1970s, the river had become one huge cesspool; an open, stinking sewer to street hawkers and squatter settlements that had mushroomed on its banks. And so, while the river supported teeming tongkang traffic on its waters, the water itself was bereft of all life.

Happy turn

Thankfully, the story doesn't end there.

Despite its sorry state, Mr Lee Kuan Yew, who was then Singapore's Prime Minister, recognised the central place the Singapore River occupied in Singapore's history, and the potential it holds as an urban, economic and identity asset in Singapore's future. So on 27 February, 1977, Mr Lee laid down the challenge to clean up the river, breathe life into it, and make it an urban asset once more; all within 10 years. Singaporeans rose to the challenge.

Beyond his wildest dreams – Shophouses at Boat Quay with prestigious commercial towers behind. Could Raffles have envisioned Singapore's success when he uttered the words: "Singapore is everything we could desire ... it will soon rise into importance"?

Photograph by *Mohd Ishak*
The New Paper

River revival – At Robertson Quay, a pleasure boat approaches the new Alkaff Bridge. River tourism was made possible after the clean-up of the river (right)

Photograph by *Jonathan Choo*
The New Paper

Sorry state – Before the big clean-up, low tide reveals the Singapore River in a desperate need of resuscitation

Photograph by *Lai Chee Weng*
URA Resource Centre

A river reborn

BY September 1987, the great Singapore River clean-up was completed.

Sewers no longer emptied their fetid contents directly into the waterway; the riverbed was dredged, and sunken boats were removed. In one month, 260 tons of rubbish was removed - about the weight of 32 elephants. Its stinking black waters became a deep green once more. And between 1986 and 1990, a million fishes - sea bass and red tilapia - and prawns were released in the Singapore River.

Joint effort

To achieve this, the concerted and coordinated efforts of a multitude of public and private sector agencies, including the URA, was required.

Learning from the examples of the Seine of Paris, and Paseo del Rio in San Antonio, Texas, among other water bodies, the URA drew up plans for the development of the river banks.

The URA published its vision for the area in its Singapore River Concept Plan in May 1985, two years ahead of the completion of the great river clean-up.

Three zones

The Singapore River Concept Plan (1985) identified three development zones along the Singapore River - Boat Quay, Clarke Quay and Robertson Quay - linked by a 15m-wide, continuous riverside promenade hugging the Singapore River's serpentine curves. These three zones will be developed as distinct areas for living, work and play while keeping a sense of history through selective conservation.

This identification of three zones serves to highlight, retain and enhance the respective identities of each zone through conservation, urban design, the optimisation of land use potential and the encouragement of suitable riverine activities.

Holistic strategy

A Development Guide Plan that focused on reviving the area through an urban design and development strategy was proposed. This strategy embraced the conservation of significant old buildings and adapting their old warehouse uses to new commercial uses like retail, entertainment and food and beverage uses.

Thus, the differing architectural identities of each of the three zones were capitalised on and proposed for new uses - restaurants, pubs and offices in Boat Quay; shops, restaurants and entertainment outlets at Clarke Quay; and homes, art establishments and hotels at Robertson Quay.

For its remarkable rebirth, the Singapore River project was placed in the Top 100 of the UN-Habitat's Dubai International Awards for Best Practices in Improving the Living Environment in 2000.

Watercolour – Pensive, pastel hues of Clarke Quay buildings reflected in the Singapore River belie the mammoth 10-year, multi-agency effort to clean it up

Photograph by *Mohd Ishak*
The New Paper

Queen of the quays

B OAT Quay used to bustle day and night with sweaty
coolies, deftly negotiating gangplanks between
tongkangs and the quay, with heavy sacks on their
tanned backs. Today, waiters negotiate crowds of
merry-makers, orders in hand. What a sea change
this most historic of the Singapore River's quays
has witnessed.

Paving the way
Boat Quay was identified as one of three development
zones of the Singapore River in URA's Singapore River
Concept Plan, published in 1985.

In order to demonstrate the Government's commitment
to not just cleaning up the river's waters but also
stimulate activities on its banks, a granite-paved mall
was completed at Boat Quay in October 1986. Its design
was inspired by the classical Chinese gardens that
Singapore's immigrant Chinese forefathers probably
knew before their diaspora.

From warehouse to public house
Then in 1989, Boat Quay became the first area on the
banks of the Singapore River to be conserved. By July1991,
restorations to about 110 privately-owned shophouses
fronting Boat Quay and Circular Road were completed,
encouraged by waivers of development charge and
car park deficiency charges.

Instead of storing rubber, rice, rattan and foodstuffs,
these historic buildings were now adapted for re-use as
trendy restaurants, pubs, and offices. The quayside itself
now supports day and night feasting, no longer a
landing place for sacks of rice and dried produce.

Quintessentially Singapore
Today, such al fresco dining on this quaint quayside
against the backdrop of the towering CBD skyscrapers,
has become part of the Singapore experience.

The historic shophouses themselves, in charming contrast
to the modern skyscrapers, are a reminder of Singapore's
not-too-distant past when the lifeblood of the nation
flowed through the Singapore River, now placid
and green.

Charm in contrast – What our forefathers built, our generation built upon (right)

Photograph by Mohd Ishak
The New Paper

Different crowd – The sound of Hokkien and Teochew (Chinese dialects) spoken by workers of the Boat Quay of old is today replaced by a gamut of international languages

Photograph by Mohd Ishak
The New Paper

Boat Quay circa 1870 and present – Still recognisable after all these years.
Thanks to the river clean-up, infrastructure upgrading and revitalisation of
activities on its banks, Boat Quay has kept up with the times

Revelry redux

ARCHITECTURALLY distinct from Boat Quay's shophouses, Clarke Quay's larger warehouses or "godowns" offer a variety of loftier spaces in addition to the typically narrow volumes of shophouses. This, and its location on the Singapore River lend a unique flavour to the ambience of Clarke Quay.

Water margin
Jutting into a meander in the river's course, Clarke Quay has a distinct waterside village atmosphere that, since its conservation and adaptive re-use, is associated with a fun and family-oriented image. Merely 20 years ago, the scene could not have been more different.

In the 1980s, Clarke Quay looked like a ghost town. The deserted, crumbling warehouses in this, the second of three development zones of the Singapore River identified in URA's Singapore River Concept Plan 1985, were a sorry sight. The edifices of the wealth of local businessmen of yore, they stood as wasted vestiges of a bygone era.

Family feasting at Clarke Quay
– Satay fires light up the brick-faced, European-styled architecture of what used to be the godown of prominent Teochew leader Lim Teck Lee (1888 - 1982), built in the 1920s (right)

Photograph by *Mohd Ishak*
The New Paper

Poo poo island – Now demolished, the building on the traffic island facing the Lim Teck Lee warehouse used to be a public toilet

Photograph by *Lai Chee Weng*
URA Resource Centre

Festival village

In July 1989, as part of its development plan for the Singapore River, the URA launched the sale of five parcels of land on this site, bounded by River Valley Road, Tan Tye Place, Clarke Quay and North Boat Quay. The brief to developers was to transform Clarke Quay into a traffic-free festival village while retaining the original architecture of more than 50 historic buildings. In 1993 when the project was completed, Clarke Quay entered a new phase of its history.

Today, life has returned to Clarke Quay. Dining, shopping and entertainment facilities are set in a bustling riverfront festival village ambience. With quayside satay fires and warmly-lit interiors of the buildings huddled tight on this river bend, and clusters of boats gently rising and falling by the bank, you can still imagine the days of early towkays like Hoo Ah Kay and Lim Teck Lee and the quayside revelry that must have gone on till late on festival nights here.

Out on a limb – Thrill-seekers get their rush at Clarke Quay's reverse bungee jump set-up (right)

Photograph by *Jonathan Choo*
The New Paper

On bended quay – Nestled between Fort Canning Park and a dogleg in the Singapore River, Clarke Quay is a waterside haven

Photograph by *Mohd Ishak*
The New Paper

Sleepy no more

FARTHERMOST upriver, Robertson Quay used to be the proverbial sleepy backwater where rotting boats and obsolete industries - boat yards, rice mills and sawmills - waited out their final days. Today, it boasts smart apartments, home offices, arts institutes and boutique hotels.

Catalysing change

Bounded by River Valley Road, Damar Road, Robertson Quay, Martin Road and Mohamad Sultan Road, Robertson Quay forms the third and largest of the three development zones under the URA's Singapore River Concept Plan 1985.

Private lands, accounting for about 65 per cent of Robertson Quay, were amalgamated for development, while the remaining state-owned lands were sold for private sector development.

Riverside scale

These developments were subject to the URA's urban design guidelines that stipulated a four-storey height along the river promenade to retain the riverside scale. Plots farther behind were allowed to be built up to 10 storeys at a maximum plot ratio of 2.8.

Unlike the developments at Boat Quay and Clarke Quay, no time frame was set for the completion of development to reflect market forces. Nevertheless, today, the quiet air of prime waterfront housing has replaced the long silence of dilapidation.

Faded façade – Remnants of the sleepy hollow that Robertson Quay once was are becoming rarer as apartments, boutique hotels and arts institutions take root (right)

Photograph by *Simon Ker*
The New Paper

Arts flavoured

This is complemented by the distinct arts ambience of Robertson Quay, where the likes of the Singapore Tyler Print Institute (STPI) and the Singapore Repertory Theatre (SRT) have sunk roots, facilitated by the URA's collaboration with the National Arts Council.

The former godown now occupied by the STPI houses a fully-equipped printmaking workshop, art gallery, and paper mill - capable of the complete range of processes from papermaking to selling the finished work of art under one roof.

The SRT, one of Asia's leading English-language theatres, stages Broadway and West End drama and musicals in its 380-seat auditorium carved out of a historic warehouse in Robertson Quay. It capitalises on its proximity with the vibrant pub strip at Mohamad Sultan Road and eateries at Robertson Walk to offer a total theatre experience by the riverside.

Art you can walk on   One of three new bridges spanning the Singapore River, the polychromatic Alkaff Bridge is irresistible to lensmen (above)

Photograph by *Casey Seyu Tzyy Wei*
Lianhe Zaobao

Stairway to haven   Robertson Quay appeals to homeowners who wish for quiet, yet close to both Orchard Road shops and CBD offices (left)

Photograph by *Jonathan Choo*
The New Paper

Going to great lengths   Boutique hotels like The Gallery Hotel in Robertson Quay stand out for the little extras like designer interiors and glass pools (right)

Photograph by *Simon Ker*
The New Paper

Walking the talk

SHARING a vision is not enough to get things moving on the ground. As it had demonstrated in catalyst projects at Boat Quay, Clarke Quay and Robertson Quay, the URA, in collaboration with its partner agencies, rolled up its sleeves and completed important infrastructural projects.

The URA's Development Guide Plan for Singapore River was released in 1994. But already in the Concept Plan 1991, the URA recognised the importance of the Singapore River area as a commercial corridor linked to Orchard Road. This vision was underscored with development guidelines for Clarke Quay and Robertson Quay, where a resident population was encouraged through the planning provision for housing to support local commerce.

Above the mark – The reconstruction and reinforcement of river walls along the Singapore River's length was a $100 million project that began in 1992

Photograph by *Simon Ker*
The New Paper

ALKAFF BRIDGE
1997

Restoring links – The restoration of historic Read Bridge (pictured), and Ord Bridge further upstream, cost $2.8 million

Photograph by *Mohd Ishak*
The New Paper

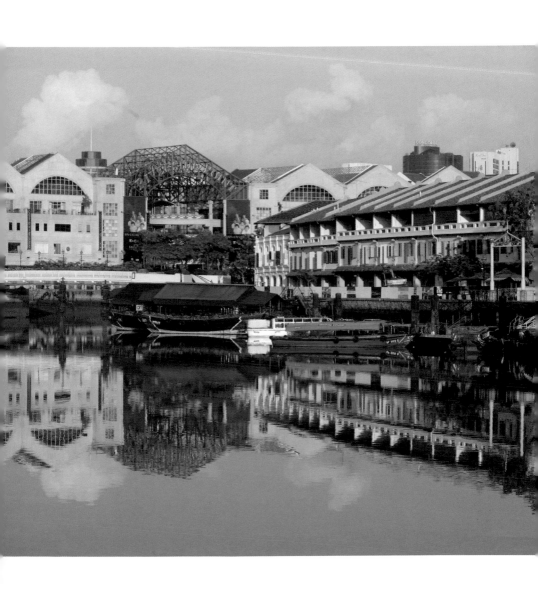

Enabling access

The Singapore River, though cleaned-up, needs constant tending. In 1992, the then Ministry of Environment implemented the URA designs for the reconstruction and fortification of the century-old river walls and quay steps, to the tune of $100 million.

These improvements allowed people to come even closer to the water's edge and provided landing points from where they can embark on scenic boat rides.

As an integral part of the urban design of the river and its environs, a continuous 6 kilometre long, tree-lined mall was built along the length of the river, linking all its three zones. This project was completed in November 1999. Pedestrians can now enjoy a continuous riverside stroll or jog, uninterrupted by vehicular traffic.

Bridging banks

To further ease connectivity, three new pedestrian bridges were built to span the river at Robertson Quay, while two of the river's nine historic bridges - the Ord and Read Bridges - have been restored at the cost of $2.8 million. In the process, Ord Bridge was raised above its original height, to allow river taxis to venture further upstream, where no large boats had ever gone before.

Today, thanks to the efforts of the Singapore Tourism Board in lighting the bridges, historic bridges like the Cavenagh, Anderson and Elgin bridges glow magnificently above the placid waters of the Singapore River at night.

Upping the ante - Boat Quay's steps were retained and raised when the promenade was constructed to ensure no flooding occurs. Solid slabs of Fujian granite was used to match the original steps

Photograph by *Mohd Ishak*
The New Paper

FOL

A photographer is able to capture a
moment that people cannot always see.

*- **Henry Callahan**,*
American photographer

04

Conservation

Life and times

H OW life has changed in the 185 years since Singapore was founded in 1819. Today, these cherubic children can look forward to a proper education and treats beyond three square meals a day. Not so in the days of these men in bronze, as their knitted brows and sinewy frames illustrate - each daily bowl of broth in their gnarled hands came only through back-breaking toil.

Their toil should not be forgotten by future generations of Singaporeans. We are reminded of the struggles our forefathers endured and overcame in building this nation and city in sculptures like this tableau at the Esplanade - Theatres on the Bay depicting two coolies eating, and "A Great Emporium" by Malcolm Koh at North Boat Quay. Historic buildings, the direct legacy of our forefathers' labour and endeavour, are another.

Early priorities

Though the benefits of conservation are clear, it was not always a viable option for a nation severely limited by its lack of land and other resources. Faced with a booming population, acute housing shortage and a lack of jobs, pragmatism prevailed for the common good of ordinary Singaporeans in the post-war years. The government's priorities were to build more housing and create more jobs. The feverish pace of development of this period saw the demolition of many old and dilapidated buildings, to be replaced by more intensive modern developments.

Roots – Children interacting with bronze statues depicting coolies eating outside the Esplanade - Theatres on the Bay

Photograph by *Long Kwok Hong*
Lianhe Zaobao

Age of conservation dawns

By the 1980s, Singapore was enjoying tremendous economic and social progress. Marina South had been reclaimed to accommodate the future growth of the city. This alleviated pressure to demolish old quarters in the city for redevelopment. With thousands of historic buildings still standing at this time, the age of active conservation had dawned in Singapore.

Between 1983 and 1986, an extensive study of the historic urban fabric of Emerald Hill, Singapore River, Chinatown, Little India and Kampong Glam was carried out. These studies culminated in 1986 when the URA unveiled the draft Master Plan for the conservation of the historic districts of Chinatown, Little India and Kampong Glam. Today, there are 67 conservation areas with 6,400 historic buildings safeguarded.

This is a thankful thing, for, in a shrinking and increasingly competitive world, the historic fabric of cities are increasingly what sets them apart from other cities as desirable homes, places of investment and tourist destinations.

Silent sentinel – Like this ancient warrior (right), conservation safeguards the authentic legacy left us by our founding forefathers
Photograph by *Jonathan Choo*
The New Paper

Big picture – With the reclamation of Marina South, the pressure to demolish historic districts adjacent to the CBD was relieved. Telok Ayer, Ann Siang Hill, Tanjong Pagar, Bukit Pasoh and Kreta Ayer could then be conserved
Photograph by *Lee Tiah Khee*
Lianhe Zaobao

6,400 buildings gazetted, and counting...

THE Conservation Plan was published in 1989 to ensure Singapore's architectural heritage would be safeguarded even as a modern city was being developed. Guidelines to involve the private sector in the conservation of their historic buildings, as well as their adaptive re-use, were introduced.

For its part, the government introduced modern infrastructure and developed pedestrian walkways and intimate open spaces to enhance the character of each conservation area. To date, 6,400 historic buildings in 67 areas have been gazetted for conservation.

Ubiquitous, yet unique

Modern as Singapore is, what makes our city unique is our historic urban fabric comprising shophouses and warehouses of the 19th and early 20th centuries. This is best appreciated by visiting any of the three major conservation areas of Chinatown, Little India and Kampong Glam. Or the outlying historic precincts and streets in areas like Geylang, Emerald Hill, Joo Chiat, Jalan Besar and Blair Road that dot the fringe areas of the city centre.

The URA will continue to study additional areas and buildings worthy of conservation. The conservation programme continues to remain relevant for two main reasons.

Restoring, reinventing – Old world charm is a premium when historic buildings are skillfully adapted to contemporary uses. The adaptive re-use of the former General Post Office to The Fullerton Hotel amply demonstrates this (right)

Photograph by *Lee Tiah Khee*
Lianhe Zaobao

Similar, singular – They present a harmonious façade, yet each shophouse is unique, as these on Mohamad Sultan Road's club strip illustrate (below)

Photograph by *Jonathan Choo*
The New Paper

Public buy-in

Firstly, conservation is important for nation-building. Through conservation, our links to our own heritage is maintained. This strengthens our roots and our sense of belonging, binding us emotionally to this place.

To facilitate greater public involvement in the conservation process, the independent Conservation Advisory Panel (CAP) was set up in June 2002, comprising members from all walks of life. Through evaluation of the feedback on conservation received, CAP has endorsed 34 conservation proposals, covering more than 1,000 buildings to date.

Since September 2003, the URA has also made a concerted effort to consult stakeholders and owners before deciding on the conservation of any building.

City charm

Secondly, old buildings add charm to our city. They offer variety in the scale, colour and texture in our urbanscape. They help make our city unique.

As time passes and the city continues to evolve, buildings which were once considered too recent for conservation will be re-evaluated. In this regard, the URA is now also actively studying significant buildings and areas built after World War II. These more recent reinforced concrete buildings were the result of a stage of economic development when Singapore was beginning to become a modern city.

The URA will also review the conservation of landmarks and buildings that were built in the last 40 years which are symbolic of a

progressive, democratic and newly-independent, multi-ethnic Singapore. They are the works of Singapore's pioneering generation of local architects who attempted to create new buildings expressing our national identity.

With the progressive conservation of such buildings, in time, Singapore's architectural and urban history will be traceable to its earliest sources seamlessly.

Taking to the streets - At dusk each day, Smith Street becomes an urban dinning room

Photograph by *Spencer Chung Kun Soon*
Lianhe Zaobao

Urban grain - Being usually surrounded by tall buildings in land-scarce Singapore, the characteristic roofscapes of conservation areas such as Tanjong Pagar (pictured) can be appreciated

Photograph by *Dennis Thong Kah Hoong*
Lianhe Zaobao

Starting out in Chinatown

H AVING retained Chinatown's architectural links with its past by gazetting its historic buildings in 1989 and drawing up guidelines for their conservation, the next step was to demonstrate how conservation makes good economic sense.

Test case
In 1987, the URA led the way by restoring 32 state-owned shophouses along Tanjong Pagar and Neil Roads as a pilot project.

The URA took a different approach in promoting conservation in Tanjong Pagar, where the shophouses were state-owned, by clearing clogged backlanes, inserting modern infrastructure and completing a pilot conservation scheme. These were completed by 1988. The URA also prepared sales plans and guidelines and sold the 38 parcels of shophouses in the area to private developers. It then guided their restoration efforts.

Different tack
The URA also restored 45 shophouses at Smith and Sago Streets. In 1990, after the restoration works were completed, 26 of these shophouses were sold under the URA's GLS programme on 99-year leases. The rest were rented out. The restored buildings were allowed a mix of traditional and new commercial uses.

These unprecedented large-scale conservation projects kick-started the ensuing wave of conservation activities by the private sector, which owns most of the 6,400 buildings gazetted for conservation in Singapore.

Organised disorder – Where once you had to negotiate between rubbish heaps amid makeshift stalls of raw and cooked food, today the pedestrianised Trengganu Street is a study in organised disorder

Photograph by *Spencer Chung Kun Soon*
Lianhe Zaobao

Crossroads of time – A newspaper vendor reminisces the changes that have taken place at the corner of Trengganu and Smith Streets, graced by the historic Lai Chun Yuen opera theatre building

Photograph by *Spencer Chung Kun Soon*
Lianhe Zaobao

Yesterday once more

Today, the conserved buildings in Chinatown have acquired a beautiful patina from age and constant habitation. And previously "new" uses have established themselves in the area alongside the traditional ones.

In collaboration with agencies like the Singapore Tourism Board, URA completed the pedestrianisation of Pagoda and Trengganu Streets. The STB has turned Smith Street into a "food street", rekindling a measure of the memories and colour of traditional outdoor eating, sans the filth and congestion of old. Today, it is abuzz with street diners and the occasional film crew shooting a new feature film or documentary.

Win some, lose some – With the conservation of Chinatown, some stalwarts, like this confectionery shop at Sago Street (right), have remained, while others have moved on to cater to new demands (above)

Photographs by *Spencer Chung Kun Soon*
Lianhe Zaobao

Just like old times – There's always a
reason to light the lanterns in Chinatown

*Photograph by Spencer Chung Kun Soon
Lianhe Zaobao*

大中國餅家

Big brio in Little India

U NLIKE Chinatown and Kampong Glam which were areas designated by Raffles as ethnic enclaves for the Chinese and Malay-Arab communities respectively, Little India sprang spontaneously to become the commercial centre of Singapore's mainly Southern Indian community.

Little India centres around Serangoon Road, which began life as "The Road Leading Across the Island" in Lt Jackson's map of 1822. It cut across an agricultural hinterland of rice, "sireh" (a leaf consumed in betel-nut culture) and vegetable gardens. These were replaced in the early 20th century with the cattle trade on which the area's prosperity was built.

Divinely detached – Surveying Little India's hoi polloi from afar

Photograph by *Casey Seyu Tzyy Wei*
Lianhe Zaobao

Bull run

By the 1940s, however, health and sanitation problems of the cattle trade led to its gradual replacement with commercial activities as the local engine of growth. The supply of water, so essential to the cattle trade, dried up as nearby swamps were drained. In its place, the historic urban fabric of Little India, as we know it today, began to be built intensively.

Despite urbanisation, vestiges of its cattle-rearing past survive in place names such as Buffalo Road, Kerbau Road and the Kandang Kerbau Children's and Women's Hospital ("kerbau" means "buffalo", and "kandang" means "cage or pen" in Malay).

Twilight town – Little India awakens from the slumber of the afternoon heat

Photograph by *Casey Seyu Tzyy Wei*
Lianhe Zaobao

Scented morning – Jasmine, lime and lotus sweeten the potpourri that is Little India

Photograph by *Casey Seyu Tzyy Wei*
Lianhe Zaobao

Sustained spontaneity

With its vibrant street life and wealth of historic urban fabric, Little India was gazetted a conservation area in 1989. As in Chinatown, the URA undertook a pilot project involving 16 shophouses at Kerbau Road to demonstrate how conservation makes for good economic sense. These restoration works were completed in 1995.

Following this pilot project, private owners of the shophouses in the area began restoring and adapting the uses of their historic properties. Successful private sector conservation projects include Little India Arcade situated strategically at the "entrance" to the historic district down Serangoon Road. Meanwhile, spontaneity continues to reign in the streets of Little India.

Same stripes, different crowd – Day and night, Little India enchants and entrances

Photographs by *Casey Seyu Tzyy Wei*
Lianhe Zaobao

Welcome to Little India – Little India Arcade in Serangoon Road
is the gateway to the conservation area which is at the heart of all
things Indian. The URA's conservation plans and guidelines were
designed to retain and enhance the area's identity

Photograph by *Casey Seyu Tzyy Wei*
Lianhe Zaobao

Kampong Glam's peaceful persuasion

KAMPONG Glam's history is as old as that of Singapore itself - it traces its origins to a village already in existence when Raffles' landing party paddled up the Singapore River for his historic landing in 1819.

Royal roots

Its name is derived from the humble "Gelam" tree which grew in abundance in the area, and whose sap was used to caulk boats built by local boat-makers. But its history is also intertwined with that of Malay royalty. The former Sultan's palace still stands today, restored as the Malay Heritage Centre.

The other important institution here is the Sultan Mosque, which also traces its origins to the Raffles era when Singapore's founder directed that a "respectable" mosque be built near the Sultan's Palace in the Malay-Arab enclave. It is no surprise then that the former palace and mosque continue to be the cultural centre of Kampong Glam, which was gazetted as a conservation area in 1989.

Pocket of history – Kampong Glam's chief charm is its quiet, unhurried ambience

Photograph by *Lim Chye Leong*
URA

Oasis – The palm-lined, pedestrianised Bussorah Street offers a picture perfect perspective of the Sultan Mosque

Photograph by *Chew Seng Kim*
The Straits Times

Pilot push

As in Boat Quay, the URA demonstrated the government's commitment to the conservation of the district through the construction of the Bussorah Street mall in 1993. And as in Chinatown and Little India, the URA helped kick-start conservation activity with two pilot projects in 1993 and 1995. The first project involved 13 shophouses in Bussorah Street, Baghdad Street and Arab Street which were completed in 1995. The second project involved 35 shophouses at Bussorah Street, with its memorable vista of the grand Sultan Mosque. It was completed in 1998.

Today, Kampong Glam's quiet charms are one of Singapore's best kept secrets, where unique products, from precious stones to rare potions of essential oils; rattan-ware to gorgeous sheer fabric, can be found.

Call to prayer – The Sultan Mosque is Singapore's pre-eminent mosque (right)

Photograph by *Chew Seng Kim*
The Straits Times

Soaring spirit – Before sleek skyscrapers like The Gateway (left of picture), the Sultan Mosque's pinnacles express the aspirations of the human spirit (left)

Photograph by *Ho Peng Yew*
Lianhe Zaobao

Best of both worlds

GOING by architectural and historical merit alone, China Square would have been a deserving case for conservation. But its size and location, right next to the CBD, meant that it carried a premium on its land value. To realise its full development potential, there was palpable pressure to level the site and build intensively on it. But this would have meant that a part of Singapore's history would have been obliterated.

Balanced approach

After carefully weighing the available strategies, the URA took the middle path - an approach which struck a balance between the options of total redevelopment and total conservation.

Only the most architecturally and historically significant buildings were conserved. This amounted to about half of the existing buildings on site, including the historic Fuk Tak Chi Temple and a Chinese school built in traditional Chinese architectural style. These conserved buildings were then parcelled together with adjacent vacant state lands for integrated conservation and new developments. This concept allowed the integration of new buildings with the historic fabric.

Pro-business statement – The PWC Building, built on a "white" site, towers above the conserved shophouses of China Square (left)

Photograph by *Jonathan Choo*
The New Paper

Hokien Street - Singapore

Vintage vista – The dilapidation of the Hokien Street of old (left) is a far-cry from today's urban contrast of new and conserved historic architecture

Photograph courtesy of *NAS*

Pedestrians rule – Glass-roofed and pedestrianised streets like Amoy Street in China Square are a hit with office workers from the neighbouring CBD and tourists (right)

Photograph by *Jonathan Choo*
The New Paper

Pro-business measures

In November 1996, the URA completed the sale of all seven land parcels in China Square for a combination of conservation and new modern developments. Being pro-business, the URA also introduced the concept of "white" sites in China Square to offer flexibility to developers. In "white" sites, the developer is empowered to decide on the mix of a range of permissible uses and the relative apportioning of space given to each use, up to the maximum gross floor area commanded by the project.

The URA also sought feedback from the public through exhibiting the planning proposal for China Square and worked closely with architects and developers to guide the urban design of the multi-faceted project. Today, China Square is the address of many home offices, creative offices and international banks.

Award winning

In 2001, the developer of Far East Square, a mixed conservation-redevelopment project within the China Square area, won the FIABCI Prix d'Excellence (Specialised Category) Award given out by the International Real Estate Federation for excellence in all real estate disciplines involved in the project's creation.

Historic half – About 50 per cent of the historic fabric in China Square that had architectural significance and structural integrity were conserved and integrated with new development

Photograph by *Jonathan Choo*
The New Paper

Where the twain meets – For its successful integration of conserved historic buildings with new development, the Far East Square project in China Square won the prestigious FIABCI Prix d'Excellence (Specialised Category) Award in 2001

Photograph by *Jonathan Choo*
The New Paper

Saving secondary settlements

THERE are singular streets and street corners in the city's surrounding suburbs whose urban identity arises from the presence of historic buildings forming the streetscape. These include the streets of such secondary settlements as Geylang, Joo Chiat, Tanjong Katong, Balestier Road, and Jalan Besar.

Unlike in Chinatown, Little India or Kampong Glam, however, the historic urban fabric in these areas do not form enough of a critical mass to be designated a conservation area. Yet, they do hold their own by way of retaining the identity of the place and are markers of social memories. These streetscapes are deserving of being conserved.

Streetscapes saved

A different conservation strategy, however, is required, one in which the rear portions of these architecturally significant buildings are allowed to be redeveloped - to the maximum height stipulated by the Master Plan plot ratio and height control.

This helps to realise the development potential of the site, while retaining the historic streetscape and scale.

Indeed, walking in these streets, pedestrians will hardly be aware of the redeveloped rear portions of the historic buildings fronting the street, as these will generally be hidden from view by the restored buildings in front.

Identity anchor – The conservation of architecturally significant streetscapes such as at Balestier Road (pictured), anchors the identities of these secondary settlements

Photograph by *Wang Hui Fen*
The Straits Times

If these walls could speak!

I F only the walls of Singapore's National Monuments could speak, they would utter volumes of the lives and times of the people who used or inhabited them, some dating almost to the very founding of Singapore by Raffles in 1819. And, though relatively youthful compared to the historic edifices in China, India or Europe, their stories would centre on the relentless cycles of change these buildings have witnessed.

House to Parliament House

Take Singapore's oldest National Monument, the Old Parliament House. This building, now used as an arts venue, was built by G D Coleman as a house for the merchant John Argyle Maxwell in 1827, just nine years after Raffles' landing. Maxwell never lived in the house, and it was rented to the government for use as the Court House before the government bought the building in 1841. The building was extended in 1875 and renovated in 1955 for use as a Council Chamber for the new Legislative Assembly and later, as Parliament House until Singapore's new Parliament House was opened in 6 September 1999.

Old Parliament House was gazetted as a National Monument in 1992. To date, 50 buildings in Singapore have been accorded this status, including the Nagore Durga Shrine (completed 1830), Jamae Mosque (1835), Thian Hock Keng Temple (1842), and Chijmes (1903).

National treasures – From top, Abdul Gafoor Mosque, Asian Civilisations Museum, Siong Lim Temple and Raffles Hotel (left)

URA Resource Centre

Drawing inspiration I – The form of the glass-clad, 52-storey Capital Tower appears to mimic the gopuram of the Sri Mariaman Temple, a National Monument (right)

Photograph by *Spencer Chung Kun Soon*
Lianhe Zaobao

Ensuring authentic restorations

All building works carried out on these gems among Singapore's historic architecture have to adhere to the strictest preservation guidelines. The URA, as the Technical Arm of the Preservation of Monuments Board (PMB), processes development applications for such works. It prepares preservation guidelines and guides their implementation on these exemplars of Singapore historic architecture. The URA also evaluates proposals for the use of donations under the Tax-Exemption Scheme.

Adapting to new uses

In 1990, Chijmes was sold under the GLS programme with guidelines provided by the URA for the sensitive conservation and adaptive re-use of the convent complex as a dining and entertainment attraction. The project was completed in 1997. Chijmes received an Award of Merit in the 2002 Asia-Pacific Heritage Conservation Awards for Culture Heritage Conservation by United Nations Educational, Scientific and Cultural Organisation (UNESCO).

Drawing inspiration II – Pointed Gothic arches at Chijmes seem purpose-designed for this model's exotic head-dress (right)

Photograph by *Ashleigh Sim*
Streats

Stately abode – The Old Parliament House, Singapore's oldest National Monument, was originally built as a private residence

Photograph courtesy of *NAS*

Award for authenticity

I T has been 15 years since the first historic districts were gazetted for conservation in 1989. Yet for the last 10 of these 15 years, the URA has been recognising excellence in conservation works with the conferment of the URA Architectural Heritage Awards (AHA).

Icing on the cake

This began with nine conservation projects, including the City Hall, Raffles Hotel and Empress Place Building, whose owners and architects were honoured with the "Good Effort" award for their conservation efforts in 1994.

The annual AHA was instituted the following year and count the River House at Clarke Quay (1995), Singapore Art Museum (1996), Chijmes (1997), Shuang Lin Monastery (1999), and Fullerton Hotel and Thian Hock Keng Temple (2001) as past winners.

Door god's new shoes – Once facing the sea and the customary thanksgiving first stop for Chinese immigrants upon arrival in Singapore, the Thian Hock Keng Temple's restoration earned it a URA Architectural Heritage Award in 2001. The National Monument was first built in 1842

Photograph by *Wang Hui Fen*
The Straits Times

Layering the cake

Since 2003, the AHA is conferred in two categories: A and B.

Category A awards are given to examples of excellent restoration work on National Monuments, conservation buildings in the historic districts such as Chinatown, Little India and Kampong Glam, as well as in Good Class Bungalow areas. The restoration of the Abdul Gafoor Mosque (2003), Empress Place Building (2003), and Old Parliament House (2004) have won Categeory A awards.

Category B awards recognise excellent examples of conservation in buildings in all other areas, including in secondary settlements like Balestier and Joo Chiat where the integration of conservation and new erection is permitted. Examples of winners include Nos 50 and 66 Emerald Hill Road (2003), and No 7 Kim Yam Road (2004).

To date, a total of 67 well-restored historic buildings have received Good Effort Awards and the AHA.

Capital gains – Detail of Raffles Hotel column. Where restoration is concerned, the devil is in the details

Photograph by *Edwin Koo*
Streats

Recognising rigour – The AHA is the badge of best practice in the restoration of Monuments like the Raffles Hotel and conservation of historic buildings such as those in Chinatown (pictured)

Photograph by *Spencer Chung Kun Soon*
Lianhe Zaobao

Jewels in the conservation crown

IF memories and memory-making are the currency of conservation, then the Raffles Hotel must be one of the bigger currency bills. For only a select few of Singapore's buildings have reputations that extend well beyond the confines of Singapore's shores. And the Raffles Hotel is one of them.

Singapore institution

Established in 1888, the hotel was originally housed in a large bungalow standing on its present site; one of 20 with large gardens and owned by Europeans, that lined Beach Road. Today's Raffles Hotel is the result of successive additions made over the 116 years of its existence. Consistent with its long history, rich with anecdotes of Empire and an illustrious guest list, the chief charm of the Raffles Hotel is its nostalgia and the atmosphere of a bygone era.

Raffles Hotel was gazetted a National Monument in 1995. Today, it is the best leisure hotel in Asia (Conde Nast Traveller British edition survey 2004).

Raffles' roots – The Raffles Hotel was founded in 1888 by a quartet of enterprising Armenian brothers; Martin, Tigran, Aviet and Arshak Sarkies. Guests, through the years, include the likes of Somerset Maughm and Michael Jackson

Photograph courtesy of *Lim Kheng Chye Collection and NAS*

Bastion of Anglophiles – In a globalised world, Raffles Hotel's inimitable allure is its nostalgia of bygone Empire (right)

Photograph by *Edwin Koo*
Streats

Doyen of hotels – The Raffles Hotel is the best leisure hotel in Asia, according to the British edition of the global travel industry benchmark Conde Nast Traveller (below)

Photograph by *Edwin Koo*
Streats

Singapore landmark

Another hotel housed in an historic building is The Fullerton Hotel. Unlike the Raffles Hotel, however, The Fullerton Hotel began life as Singapore's General Post Office building in 1928 in the Neo-Classical style favoured for secular public buildings at the time. In its history, it had also housed the Exchange, the Chamber of Commerce, the Singapore Club and the Inland Revenue Authority of Singapore.

With its handsome architecture and location on the urban waterfront of the CBD, the URA saw the potential of the Fullerton Building to be developed into a special hotel. In October 1997, the URA sold it together with a reclaimed waterfront land parcel fronting Marina Bay. The development also included an underground carpark and pedestrian linkway from the Fullerton Building to the waterfront land at Marina Bay.

Following its sale, the URA chaired a supervisory design panel to guide the conservation and redevelopment of the historic landmark into a five-star hotel. It opened its doors as a hotel, The Fullerton Hotel, in December 2000.

The awards for this gorgeous conservation cum conversion project soon came. In 2001, it was awarded a URA Architectural Heritage Award. And in 2003, The Fullerton Hotel's developer clinched the international FIABCI Prix d'Excellence Award (leisure category) for its successful adaptive re-use from post office to hotel.

Doyenne of hotels – Set like a jewel on Singapore's glittering CBD seafront, The Fullerton Hotel is poised to assume its place among the world's beloved "grande hotels" (left and above)

Photograph by *Ng Sor Luan*
Streats

Photograph by *Ho Peng Yew*
Lianhe Zaobao

FOL

While there is perhaps a province in which the photograph can tell us nothing more than what we see with our own eyes, there is another in which it proves to us how little our eyes permit us to see.

*- **Dorothea Lange**,*
American photographer

105

Golden Shoe

Heart of business

THE growth of the Golden Shoe, Singapore's CBD, mirrors the dynamism of Singapore's economic and urban development. This is demonstrated by the spectacular sprouting of the skyscrapers here over the last 30 years that are now synonymous with Singapore's distinctive skyline.

But the city slate that the newly self-governing Singapore inherited in 1959 from the British wasn't a clean one. Indeed, the city centre was chockfull of dilapidated, small-scale buildings that were grossly overcrowded. Had they been allowed to remain, these buildings would have choked off any possibility of large-scale, intensive developments that were needed.

Rewriting the script

It was clear to the new government that a new script had to be written if Singapore's future as a business, commercial and financial hub was to be realised. In 1966, the formation of the Urban Renewal Department (URD) put a firm focus on solving the problems of the Central Area.

From the outset, to achieve its twin objectives of social and environmental improvement and generating economic growth, the URD emphasised close government-private sector collaboration. The government's role was to prepare a Master Plan, clear slums, amalgamate lands, insert infrastructure, provide planning and urban design guidelines, and release the lands for private development on fixed term leases.

High profile – The boundary of the Golden Shoe is instantly discernable from the air, differentiated from the fine-grain historic districts by building footprint and height. Such large-scale developments in the Golden Shoe were made possible by assembling small lots for redevelopment as amalgamated sites

Photograph by *Lee Tiah Khee*
Lianhe Zaobao

"Golden Shoe"

The URD proceeded to draw the boundary of a new CBD, whose eventual shape inspired newspaper editors to coin the term "Golden Shoe".

The development of the Golden Shoe was largely carried out under the Government Land Sales (GLS) programme, which empowered the URD and its successor from 1974, the URA, to clear and assemble small plots to sell as amalgamated lands for modern, large-scale developments.

In 1968, the second GLS programme focused on office developments with five of the six sites on offer located in Shenton Way. With the independently-developed Development Bank of Singapore (DBS) building at the Maxwell Road end, the sale of these five sites kick-started the growth of the Golden Shoe, which was destined to become the most highly prized 35 hectares of commercial real estate in Singapore.

The rest, as they say, is history.

Bold new script – The spectacular skyline of Singapore's CBD is the result of a bold rewriting of the plans inherited from the British colonial government

Photograph by *Ho Peng Yew*
Lianhe Zaobao

Photograph by *Lai Chee Weng*
URA Resource Centre

Metromorph I – The Yueh Hai Ching Temple remains (below), but its old neighbours along Philip Street (seen in this 1970 photo, left) are no more

Photograph by *Ng Chor Seng*
URA

Vertical marathon

TODAY, Singapore is a global player in banking and finance. You only have to visit the Golden Shoe to witness all the action taking place in the banking and financial institutions located here. Not surprisingly, over the years, the prestigious skyscrapers these institutions built vied vigorously for the title of "tallest building".

For years before the birth of the Golden Shoe, the two tallest buildings here were the art deco era Bank of China and Asia Insurance buildings.

Tallest - for now

With the intensification of land use for Raffles Place to a plot ratio of an average of 13.86, taller buildings began to be built. This high plot ratio was justified with the development of the MRT line and Raffles Place MRT station, which efficiently transports the increased traffic generated by such developments.

In 1974, the first United Overseas Bank (UOB) Tower took over the title of "tallest building", standing at 38 storeys. Two years later, the Oversea-Chinese Banking Corporation (OCBC) built its 52-storey OCBC Centre just off Raffles Place. It was the tallest building in Singapore, and indeed, Southeast Asia at the time.

Breaching 280m

In 1988, the 66-storey Overseas Union Bank (OUB) Centre opened at the prestigious address of 1, Raffles Place. Standing all of 280m tall, the maximum height allowable, it was the tallest building in the world outside the USA. On rainy days, occupants of its highest floors would literally dwell among the clouds.

Tallest then – Former "tallest buildings" in Singapore: the Asia Insurance Building (top) and the Bank of China Building (above)

Photographs by *Lai Chee Weng*
URA Resource Centre

Riding high – On still days, the height of the CBD towers is doubled (right)

Photograph by *Mohd Ishak*
The New Paper

Other notable CBD towers completed at this time were the 48-storey Singapore Land Tower (known then as Shell Tower), the 34-storey SingTel Exchange building and the 41-storey Six Battery Road.

The early 1990s saw two other skyscrapers join the OUB Centre at the rarified height of 280m above sea level - the UOB Plaza (1992) and Republic Plaza (1995).

Likewise, the western end of the Golden Shoe also witnessed a mushrooming of corporate towers beginning with the DBS Bank, CPF Building and International Plaza, rising 50-storeys. This group now includes the 52-storey Capital Tower, Temasek Tower (37 storeys), Fuji Xerox (former IBM) Tower (38 storeys) and 78, Shenton Way (34 storeys). The distinctive Singapore skyline thus took shape, reflecting the vibrancy of its financial and commercial life.

Spreading south

Just as, in the 1960s, the script was re-written for the redevelopment of the CBD, today, a new strategy of growth for the 21st century has been devised. The name of that strategy is Downtown at Marina Bay (DTMB).

In August 2002, the URA announced plans for a large, integrated business and financial centre at DTMB to be developed by a single master developer under a flexible development approach. The first building on this new tract of reclaimed land forming Singapore's new urban waterfront, Marina Bay, has been completed. This year, the 32-storey NTUC Headquarters was opened amid fanfare and fireworks.

Building boom – This 1980s photograph shows the flurry of construction activity taking place at the junction of Cantonment and Anson Roads at the western end of the Golden Shoe

Photograph courtesy of
Chu Sui Mang Collection and NAS

Photograph by *Lai Chee Weng*
URA Resource Centre

Metromorph II – The Straits Trading Building (below)
sits on the site of the fomer Medical Hall at Battery Road,
seen in this 1966 photo (right)

Photograph by *Ng Chor Seng*
URA

Guided growth

A key function of urban design is to ensure that the city's overall scale is moderated harmoniously. Another is to ensure that buildings offer a consistent standard of urban amenity, such as covered walkways, landscaping, and sidewalks. At the same time, the optimal realisation of the development potential of the land must be achieved.

In the Golden Shoe, a clear demonstration of urban design in action can be observed. The invisible hand that guides height control, for instance, can be seen in the "urban cascade" visible from Ann Siang Hill. The greatly contrasting scales of the skyscrapers of Raffles Place and that of the restored historic shophouses in Telok Ayer is moderated by the middling-height office buildings along Robinson Road and Shenton Way.

Singapore's Wall Street

Shenton Way was conceived as Singapore's Wall Street. The fact that much of Shenton Way was unencumbered reclaimed land allowed developments there to be effectively shaped by urban design guidelines. These guidelines were incorporated in the conditions of the sales of these sites.

The urban design guidelines here specified a podium and tower typology, with the podium height capped at four storeys to create a strong and human-scaled street edge. As was introduced by Raffles more than 100 years before for shophouses, each new development in the CBD had to provide covered walkways, with the soffit heights controlled for visual continuity between different developments.

Plot ratio was calculated on the basis of the capacity of the MRT and road networks, and the volume of pedestrian and vehicular traffic the buildings would attract. Today gross plot ratio (GPR) stands at a maximum of 12.6-plus in Raffles Place, the "plus" varying from site to site. On average, the resultant GPR is 13.86.

City in a garden

Recognising the importance of greenery in an urban setting, it was a requirement from the onset that 2 per cent of the development cost of each building was to be spent on landscaping. This resulted in indoor art and roof gardens being provided in these buildings.

Pushing boundaries – Today's CBD stands largely on reclaimed land, with successive efforts pushing the seafront from Telok Ayer Street (as seen in the photograph circa 1870) to Raffles Quay-Shenton Way less than 100 years later. Tomorrow's CBD, to be built in Downtown at Marina Bay, continues this seaward expansion (right and below)

Photograph courtesy of *Singapore History Museum*
National Heritage Board

Photograph by *Lim Chye Leong*
URA

Since the CBD has a southern sea frontage, sea views for each development was also safeguarded by the careful placement of the tower blocks atop the podiums. In the early days, planners actually went out to sea regularly to check on this.

Bustling 24/7

To keep the streets bustling into the night, mixed-use developments were encouraged by allowing the residential component to be exempt from development charge and plot ratio calculations. But this measure turned out to be insufficient to generate a critical mass of residents in the city.

In the near future, more people will live in the city when projects like The Pinnacle@Duxton and Icon are completed.

Metromorph IV – Robinson Road, near Lau Pa Sat, used to be lined with three-storey shophouses as seen in this 1970 photo (below), replaced today by high-rise office blocks (right)

Metromorph III – Cheang Hong Lim Place (1970 photo, above left) is now a welcoming pocket of greenery in the heart of the Golden Shoe (above)

Invisible influence – The hand of urban design is revealed in the urban cascade from the 280m-high skyscrapers of Raffles Place, through the middling-height towers of Shenton Way and Robinson Road, to the two and three-storey conserved shophouses of Telok Ayer (right)

Urban stage

A NYONE who arrives at Raffles Place would feel it:
The urge to look up and marvel at the ring of
skyscrapers surrounding the urban space. You would then
scan the landscaped plaza for some eye-catching activity
taking place at ground level. Or simply choose to linger
awhile to people-watch, for this urban space is hardly ever
empty of people. Welcome to Raffles Place.

Majestic

Here, you can't miss a sense of Singapore's financial and
commercial clout. Sharp-suited executives scurrying across the
plaza complement the resplendent aluminium and granite-clad
commercial towers in this, the heart of Singapore's banking and
financial centre. Product launches and advertising campaigns,
corporate charity events and flag sellers all strut their stuff here,
and their attention-grabbing antics add to the buzz of the
hoi polloi.

Historic

But there is also a hint of history here. The plaster facades of
the Raffles Place MRT station are reduced-scale reminders of
the former John Little's departmental store, a local landmark.
And how many generations have associated this very space
with the vibrancy of Singapore's commerce? After all ,
Raffles Place, since the time of Raffles when it was known as
Commercial Square, has always been an urban stage upon
which the play of commercial growth has been enacted
through the ages. No doubt, this will continue far into
the future.

What's the buzz? – Product launch,
charity event, publicity stunt - something's
always afoot at Raffles Place

Photograph by *Terence Tan*
The Straits Times

Pulse of business – The suit styles may have changed, but Raffles Place has been at the heart of big business in Singapore since Raffles' time

Photograph by *Terence Tan*
The Straits Times

Walking under cover

Y OU may take the humble five-footway for granted in daily life. But try to imagine Singapore without this ubiquitous urban element. Suddenly, its practical value - providing a pedestrian-only accessway and shielding them from the sun and rain - becomes patently clear.

Kaki lima

The shophouse covered walkway, or five-footway, which originated from the Malay term "kaki lima", has been interpreted in many ways throughout its history. Even among Singapore's historic buildings, the scale of five-footways differed. In modest shophouses of Kampong Glam, for instance, you might have to watch your head as you walk down a five-footway.

In historic commercial buildings in town, such as the Asia Insurance Building, the five-footway took on loftier proportions befitting its urban locale. This urban scale is continued in the proportions of five-footways required of new buildings in the Golden Shoe. Today, new covered walkways along the front of the buildings are required to provide at least a 45 degree overhang, to provide sufficient shade and shelter from sun and rain.

Photograph courtesy of *NAS*

Changed alley – Change Alley, with its three levels of shops and airy atrium is the ultimate incarnation of the former haunt of numismatic collectors (left and above)

Photograph by *Terence Tan*
The Straits Times

Changing fortunes

A variant of the covered walkway was the Change Alley of old, famous among both locals and tourists. It used to be a congested alley chockfull of cheap trinket stalls and makeshift numismatic merchants - hence its name. The old Change Alley was demolished and incorporated with the $600 million Caltex House development. When it returned in 1994, the alley was transformed into a three-storey shopping galleria linking Raffles Place and Collyer Quay, with direct access to the underground Raffles Place MRT station.

Urban de rigueur – From the poshest of hotels, like the Raffles Hotel, to the humblest of shophouses, the five-footway is customary (right)

Photograph by *Edwin Koo*
Streats

Grateful shade – Singapore would be a very different city if not for the rain- and sun-shading five footway which Raffles introduced here (bottom right)

Photograph by *Spencer Chung Kun Soon*
Lianhe Zaobao

Urban fixture – It may no longer measure 5 feet wide and glass and granite may have replaced the timber and terracotta of old shophouses, but the five-footway remains relevant to urban life in Singapore (below)

Photograph by *Spencer Chung Kun Soon*
Lianhe Zaobao

Going underground

W ITH the advent of escalators, the logical next step in pedestrianisation was to have underground or overhead pedestrian connectors that could cross lines of vehicular traffic. This would provide for seamless pedestrian access to inter-connected buildings. This possibility was capitalised on when Singapore's MRT system was being planned and built.

Linked to 36 buildings

Working closely with its partner agencies such as the Land Transport Authority (LTA), the URA ensured that knock-out panels were pre-installed in the underground stations so that when adjacent buildings were developed, these panels could be removed, and (voila!) people would have seamless underground access to the new building. As a result of such forward planning, for instance, today you can walk comfortably either underground or under-cover above ground, from Raffles Place MRT Station to 36 buildings in the surrounding area.

Underground bustle

Previously, pedestrians were subject to the vicissitudes of the weather when walking from Raffles City to Marina Square. Today, there is an underground air-conditioned shopping and dining experience, thanks to CityLink Mall. The Esplanade - Theatres on the Bay and all the developments at Marina Centre are accessible via CityLink Mall.

Way to go

This is a taste of things to come as Singapore continues to be a more pedestrian-friendly country. In the Downtown at Marina Bay, for instance, people will have pedestrian access to the extensive array of amenities via travellators, direct MRT access, covered walkways and underground malls.

Here's looking at you – Commuters dashing to their destinations via direct underground links from MRT stations hardly notice the larger-than-life murals of themselves

Photograph by *Terence Tan*
Lianhe Zaobao

Escalated elation – Emerging from CityLink Mall into a sunset street, a couple share a private moment (above)

Photograph by *Spencer Chung Kun Soon*
Lianhe Zaobao

Serene splendour – With pedestrian traffic routed underground to CityLink Mall, the War Memorial Park is an oasis of calm in the heart of the city (right)

Photograph by *Spencer Chung Kun Soon*
Lianhe Zaobao

Life underground – Finding private space in a public realm at the underground CityLink Mall (below)

Photograph by *Spencer Chung Kun Soon*
Lianhe Zaobao

FOL

Photography is more than an art.
Photojournalism is knowledge.

- Tukiman Warji,
Berita Harian photojournalist

06

Honing on quality

Home improvement

HOME ownership among Singaporeans is among the highest in the world, thanks to the availability of affordable, good quality public housing. Still, it is only human nature to aspire for more.

This aspiration has been continuously addressed in the URA's successive Concept Plans which promise a more livable city with a wide choice of housing locations and housing types.

New sites and building types
The URA has been addressing such aspirations since its inception in 1974, soon after which it paved the way for condominium housing. Provisions for other housing types followed, including cluster housing, strata bungalows and city living.

Over the last 30 years, new prime housing areas have been successfully created out of lands which were used for outmoded industries. There is also a shift towards housing in the city centre so as to create a downtown buzz befitting a 24/7 metropolis.

Returning to the city
People who enjoy living amid the buzz of the city will have their wishes come true as more homes are built in the city in the future. In the Concept Plan 2001, 90,000 more units of housing will be added to the existing 30,000 in the city, raising the resident city population from 3 to 7 per cent. These will mostly be located at the Downtown at Marina Bay, where new high-rise apartments overlooking urban greenery will be introduced.

If the take-up rate seen at the November 2001 launch of Icon, a downtown private housing project, and The Pinnacle@Duxton, a public housing project launched this year, is anything to go by, the city will be that much more vibrant after hours.

Living the high life
At present, only about 35,000 people live above the 20th storey. This is set to rise with housing blocks taller than 30 storeys allowed in areas with less height restrictions.

For instance, the 1,848-unit The Pinnacle@Duxton will rise 50 storeys. At the Downtown at Marina Bay, a new housing tower, The Sail, will shoot 70-storeys into the sky. Now, that's living it up.

Addressing aspirations – Condominiums, such as River Place (pictured) are a winning formula in balancing eficient land use with trappings of the resort lifestyle

Photograph by *Lee Tiah Khee*
Lianhe Zaobao

Creating a new 'C'

FACT or myth, Singaporeans are said to desire the five "Cs" - career, car, cash, credit card, and condo. Indeed, condominiums are such an integral part of the Singaporean psyche that it is hard to imagine a time when there were no such developments here - until the URA introduced this housing form with its guidelines for condominium housing.

The 1979 completion of Singapore's first condominium, Pandan Valley, was quickly followed by the likes of Grangeford, Horizon Towers and Arcadia condominiums. The age of condominiums, whose popularity continues till today, had dawned.

A winning formula

The reasons for the popularity of condominiums are no mystery: they address the rising aspirations of Singaporeans for a higher quality of housing with direct access to recreational facilities, as an alternative to landed property. Condominium housing, which combines a high-density housing model with shared facilities for the country club lifestyle, thus became a winning formula.

Sites for condominiums close to established housing estates were also made available. The Trellis Towers development at Toa Payoh is one example of a new condominium development near a mature public housing estate to introduce more new homes there.

Eye on the good life – Singaporeans' eyes were opened to the good life that condominium living offered with early examples such as The Arcadia (below and right)

Photographs by *Lee Tiah Khee*
Lianhe Zaobao

A lot to call your own

IN June 1993, the URA introduced the sale of small landed housing sites for development by small developers and individuals through the release of such sites at Kew Drive. This follows the aim of the Concept Plan 1991 to provide more opportunities for Singaporeans to enjoy medium and low density private housing.

The current Concept Plan 2001 aims to provide even more low and medium-rise private housing, even for a projected population of 5.5 million.

More variety of housing types

Aside from offering a range of housing densities, a greater variety of housing forms was also studied. In April 1990, the Ministry of National Development launched a concept competition to tap ideas from private architects and developers. Three sites were offered - in Newton Road, University Road and Hillview Avenue.

The result was a slew of new housing concepts, including strata bungalows and cluster housing with gardens, swimming pools or tennis courts shared between them. Both of these new housing forms combine the best of landed and condominium living in one development. The URA adopted these new housing forms and detailed guidelines were issued. The result are developments such as the Teneriffe,a cluster housing project, and Tudor Ten, a strata bungalow development.

My-ville, Singapore – Small developers, including individual owner-developers, were the target audience of the land sales at Kew Drive and Eastwood estates (above and next page)

Photograph by *Ho Peng Yew*
Lianhe Zaobao

More flexible guidelines

Besides exploring new housing forms, the URA also reviewed guidelines for private housing and set more flexible standards to encourage greater creativity and better utilisation of land.

Smaller plot sizes were allowed for semi-detached houses and a smaller setback from the road was required. Despite smaller plots, a slew of recent housing projects have demonstrated that innovative architecture can still be created, through the clever manipulation of the available space to introduce light, air, ventilation and interesting spaces in the dwellings. This includes the use of architectural devices such as vertical gardens and "borrowed space".

Photograph by *Ho Peng Yew*
Lianhe Zaobao

From dirt to riches

W HO says you can't have your cake and eat it too? In February 1993, the URA with its public sector partners, embarked on an initiative at the Bukit Timah-Hillview area to achieve a dual purpose - relocate pollutive industries and free the land for condominium housing.

With the enthusiastic participation of the private sector land owners and developers, the project was a resounding success and earned a place among the Global Top 100 of the Dubai International Awards for Best Practices in Improving the Living Environment in 1998. The secret in this successful recipe lay in unlocking the inherent value of the land and adding a sweetener to the relocation deal.

Making $ense

As a natural extension of the prime Bukit Timah residential corridor, the rezoning of the area from industrial to residential use unlocked the inherent value of the land, which was largely on desirable freehold or 999-year leases.

To sweeten the deal, owners of the 118 industrial sites were incentivised with an additional plot ratio of 0.3 if they converted their land from industrial to residential use within three to five years from 1993. This meant they could build more apartments on the land, further enhancing the land value. The development charge usually tied to plot ratio enhancements was also waived.

These measures proved instrumental in freeing 118 hectares of prime land (half the size of Toa Payoh) for the development of about 10,000, mostly freehold, condominium units.

Win-win-win – The twin successes in Hillview and Upper Bukit Timah of creating prime housing land while relocating pollutive industries was topped by winning the Global Top 100 of the Dubai International Awards for Best Practices in Improving the Living Environment in 1998

Photograph by *Joyce Fang*
The Straits Times

Synergy paid off

Like the Singapore River clean-up, the Bukit Timah-Hillview rezoning initiative was an example of successful multi-agency collaboration towards a common national objective. While the URA worked on planning issues, the Pollution Control Department of the then Ministry of the Environment (ENV) helped to identify the pollutive and hazardous industries. The Economic Development Board worked with Jurong Town Corporation to offer new premises for the relocated industries. And the then Public Works Department ensured that enough roads were built for the increased local population of the area.

Historic setting - Condominiums rise next to the historic, art deco-styled Ford Factory in Upper Bukit Timah where the Japanese surrender was enacted at the close of World War II

Photograph by *Joyce Fang*
The Straits Times

From backwater to prime real estate

LIVING on the seashore is one of the hallmarks of island living. In October 1996, the URA joined forces with the Housing & Development Board to promote the charms of waterfront living at Punggol 21 town.

Before Punggol 21, the URA had led a multi-agency effort to transform Tanjong Rhu from an old shipyard strip to prime private waterfront housing in the late 1980s. This was done through reclamation, master planning, urban design, sale of sites and infrastructural improvements.

Peaceful lookout point

Tanjong Rhu ("Casuarina Point" in Malay) was also known as "Sandy Point" in the early 19th century. As a natural landing point for the wooden boats of yore, it was a natural place of habitation for the early settlers of Singapore.

But after 150 years of unbridled development, it had become, by the 1980s, a strip of unkempt shipyards and squatters. URA's vision was to transform Tanjong Rhu into an enclave of good quality housing fronting the cleaned-up Kallang Basin, complete with a promenade, commercial village and recreational activities to take advantage of the unique setting.

Pollutive shipyards moved

The realisation of this vision involved persuading existing land owners to relocate their incompatible shipyard and warehousing businesses for the land to be redeveloped for residential use via the GLS programme. The process also involved the injection of infrastructure, and the reclamation of 5.6 hectares of land to form a more regular coastline which eased the flow of water. URA's planning and urban design guidelines helped shape the different developments into a harmonious whole.

Today, strolling on the promenade at sunset or enjoying the riverine view from the new lookout point or bridge, you are transported to the peace and serenity of the Tanjong Rhu of old.

Bridging dreams – A clean Kallang River, prime property at Tanjong Rhu,
a photogenic moment – the stuff of dreams come true

Photograph by *Spencer Chung Kun Soon*
Lianhe Zaobao

Sandy Point revisited – From this idyllic sandy spit, you could see the spire of St Andrew's Cathedral and Fort Canning, as shown in this sepia wash from 1847. Today, residents have a front row view of the towers of Suntec City and the CBD beyond

Photograph courtesy of *NUS Museums
National University of Singapore*

Across the water – A quiet residential quarter with a view of the city across Kallang River

Photograph by *Lee Tiah Khee
Lianhe Zaobao*

Damsel in de-stress – Not so long ago, she might have swooned from the distressing stench emanating from the polluted Kallang River

Photograph by *Spencer Chung Kun Soon*
Lianhe Zaobao

FOL

The camera makes everyone a tourist in other people's reality, and eventually in one's own.

Susan Sontag
- American essayist

O7

Working smart

New ways of working

WORKING smart is about delivering productivity with panache, while maintaining a balanced lifestyle. This, so that we can keep ahead of the curve and be globally competitive, yet enjoy the fruits of our labour in good health, quality time with family, and recreational and spiritual pursuits.

Though city planning may seem far removed from this daily balancing act, in reality, it is intimately tied with it. After all, planning decisions ultimately impinge on everyday aspects of life, from creating job opportunities, to the means of commuting to work every day.

More jobs, better environments

The current Concept Plan, published by the URA in 2001, made provisions for Singapore to be a city driven by cutting-edge technology and high value-added industries and services. This means that sufficient land has been set aside for the growth, of land-hungry but high yielding industries.

To enhance flexibility for businesses and create jobs in enriching environments, new zoning systems were introduced in the Concept Plan 2001. Recognising the need for land use planning to respond quickly and proactively to changing business needs, new "impact-based" business zones termed B1 (non-pollutive) and B2 (pollutive) have been created.

A new "white zone" has also been created to allow all uses except pollutive ones, so as to encourage a greater mix of uses under the same roof - commercial, office, residential, recreational and community spaces.

Conveniences sans commute - More facilities have been established in the regional centres at Woodlands (right), Tampines (next page) and Jurong East

Photograph by *Mohd Ishak*
The New Paper

Commuting $ensibly

Locating industries and offices close to MRT stations also entice more people to take public transport and walk to their work places. The provision of efficient and affordable transportation infrastructure is a key focus. In the Concept Plan 2001, new orbital and radial rail lines are proposed to enhance the commuting experience, even as such commuting is minimised with the introduction of regional, sub-regional and fringe centres to bring your office to your local area.

Spoilt for choice

Today, workers and employers alike can choose from a variety of alternative working environments to suit their needs. These include resort-like business parks and historic conservation buildings. And some might even choose to work from home with the new Home Office scheme offered by the HDB and URA.

Photograph by *Ho Peng Yew*
Lianhe Zaobao

Comprehensive coverage – Shops, eats, reads
- your neighbourhood spread is as good as it gets

Photograph by *Ho Peng Yew*
Lianhe Zaobao

A workplace near you

THESE days, you can shop and work near your home, thanks to the "constellation plan" introduced in the URA's Concept Plan 1991.

This was a major departure from the previous Concept Plan 1971, where businesses were encouraged to be concentrated in the Central Area, resulting in people- and vehicle-jams in the city during peak hours.

Regional centres

To position Singapore as a global financial centre, the ground-breaking Concept Plan 1991 proposed that the Central Area remains the nexus for major commercial, banking and financial activities. This continues to be the policy in the current Concept Plan 2001.

Office, shopping, recreation and food facilities will be decentralized to regional centres located about 13km from the CBD. The regional centres at Tampines, Woodlands, and Jurong East are currently in various stages of growth.

Sub-regional, fringe centres

For an even better spread, five smaller sub-regional centres at Buona Vista, Bishan, Serangoon, Paya Lebar and Marine Parade are being developed. With the exception of Marine Parade, these centres are all near MRT stations.

In addition, smaller fringe centres at Novena, Newton and Lavender have also been established. Novena Square was the first parcel at the Novena fringe centre that was sold by URA in December 1996 for a commercial development to be integrated with Novena MRT station.

Walking to work – This has become a reality for thousands living around the regional, sub-regional and fringe centres Tampines (above) and Marine Parade (next page)

Photographs by *Ho Peng Yew*
Lianhe Zaobao

Closer to you

The latest Concept Plan 2001 proposes to continue the drive to provide more jobs closer to homes. In addition to bringing more workplaces to the North, North-east and East regions, it also means building more housing in the West and in the city, so that more people can live closer to their workplaces.

The main advantage of this decentralisation plan is clear: The CBD would be less congested. And heartlanders won't have to travel too far to get from home to work and play every day.

Photograph by *Lee Tiah Khee*
Lianhe Zaobao

Noteworthy – Busker at Tampines regional centre. Everyone benefits from a shorter commute (right)

Photograph by *Ho Peng Yew*
Lianhe Zaobao

Home sweet office

A N invisible line divides this flat into a home and an office. Indeed, this renovated HDB flat is both a home and an office, a relatively new phenomenon in the heartlands.

The ability to work from the comfort of home also means more contact time with family. It is a dream come true for the more than 11,400 people who have had their home office applications approved since the scheme was jointly launched by the URA and HDB in June 2003. Of these 10,700 are for HDB flats and 700 are for private properties.

Boon to start-ups

Indeed, working from home became a reality for some as early as November 2001, when the URA launched a pilot home office scheme to allow small businesses to operate from homes in selected mixed-use zones.

The Home Office Scheme is a boon to would-be entrepreneurs, working mothers, and others who need to keep an eye on the home front while working. Such people like the flexibility to conduct businesses such as IT consultancies, architecture, advertising and real estate services from their homes.

Best of all, home offices mean lower start-up business costs and savings in commuting time and expenses. To help these home office businesses formulate longer term business plans, the approved period was extended from one year to three years from 10 June 2004.

Invisible line – This side of the curtain is the office; that side is the home - HDB apartment cum architect's office

Photograph by *Stephanie Yeow*
The Straits Times

Kitty needn't be lonely – Sohos are popular for working mothers, would-be entrepreneurs in IT, web services, advertising and real estate, and those who need to keep an eye on the home front while working

Photograph by *Stephanie Yeow*
The Straits Times

Purpose-built Sohos

As the home office concept gains popularity, new housing developments are offering built-in features that support working from home. In effect, these are purpose-built Sohos.

The Soho@Central project, another URA sales of sites project due for completion in 2008, is among the first of such purpose-built home office developments. Built over the Clarke Quay MRT station, it houses 227 column-free, high-ceilinged home office-units measuring an average 59 square metres, designed for dual flexibility as homes and offices.

Further upriver, there's The Pier At Robertson, which boasts standard smart-home technologies including the use of Internet-enabled smart phones and the security of a biometric fingerprint system for on-line financial transactions. Such provisions will certainly help make it a breeze to run a business from home.

Heartland hit – More than 90 per cent of the approved applications for Sohos came from HDB dwellers

Photograph by *Casey Seyu Tzyy Wei*
Lianhe Zaobao

Brainstorm over breakfast

EVER noticed that your best ideas come during a jog, in the shower or over a cuppa?

Early on, architects in Silicon Valley in the USA recognised this and designed buildings where the workroom is really the recreation space and vice versa. They designed corridors for chance meetings and discussions, cafes for doing Internet research and gyms for working out the brains.

Silicon Valley, Singapore-style

Likewise, in Singapore, cutting-edge research is taking place in business parks where the conventional idea of working spaces is turned on its head. And where architecture promotes synergy between some of the best brains in the world, by encouraging interaction and an exchange of ideas.

Working closely with the Jurong Town Corporation (JTC), the URA designated the first two business parks at Science Park I and II in Pasir Panjang to be near institutions of higher learning at Kent Ridge. The International Business Park next to Jurong East

regional centre and the Changi Business Park next to the Changi Airport followed.

The provision for a technology corridor from Jurong to the edge of the Central Area, made in the Concept Plan 1991, is being developed. The latest development in this zone is One-North, a 200 hectare site in central Singapore. It is being developed by JTC in three phases over the next 20 years.

The dynamic new architecture there, set amidst existing old buildings, mature trees and winding roads aims to offer spaces for serenity and mental stimulation. It is a vibrant environment in which to brainstorm and conceive, test-bed and implement innovative ideas.

Conduits of conception – Corridors, bridges, courtyards: these are the latest laboratories for generating and mulling over ideas

Photograph by *Stephanie Yeow*
The Straits Times

Breaking bread, hatching ideas – Hard at work over a meal, the denizens of Biopolis know no boundaries for idea-making

Photograph by *Stephanie Yeow*
The Straits Times

No right angles, only creative ones –
Dynamic architecture at One North
engenders out-of-the-box approaches

Photograph by *Stephanie Yeow*
The Straits Times

When 'old' = 'happening'

WALK down the quaint five-footways of Ann Siang Hill, Joo Chiat or Kandahar Street and you'll notice the smart signboards of stylish offices dealing with design, IT, media or advertising.

In the intensively competitive environment of these creative businesses, you leverage on what advantage you have to stand out and be seen and heard. A distinctive office in a conserved historic building can certainly help to raise your business profile.

Guaranteed unique

In guiding the conservation of Singapore's historic buildings, the URA upholds the "3-R Principle" of maximum retention,

sensitive restoration and careful repair. In this way, the original design of each historic building is ensured and offices in conserved buildings can justifiably boast truly unique environments - a rare commodity in the age of undifferentiated spaces offered in run-of-the-mill office towers.

Besides being architecturally unique, there's nothing like a sense of history and being in a carefully crafted building to help the creative juices flow. It is no accident that the world over, many creative businesses pick restored buildings as their workspace of choice, paying a premium for the privilege.

Welcome to my (creative) world – Your clients are primed for a different perspective right from the start

Photograph by *Spencer Chung Kun Soon*
Lianhe Zaobao

The rest is history – An architect's modern office occupies the historic setting of a conserved shophouse (above)

Photograph by *Stephanie Yeow*
The Straits Times

Pliant as bamboo – Historic buildings are versatile and can be adapted for myriad uses (right)

Photograph by *Stephanie Yeow*
The Straits Times

Ramp up on land use

Direct delivery – Multi-level vehicular access for an under-one-roof car services experience (above)

One up on flatted factories – The use of vehicular ramps makes the good idea of flatted factories even better (right)

Drive right in – AMK AutoPoint is Singapore's first multi-storey motor workshop complex offering direct vehicular access to every one of the 113 units spread over five floors (below)

Photographs by *Tukiman Warji*
Berita Harian

THOUGH they may require large amounts of precious land, the current Concept Plan 2001 makes provisions for high value-added industries such as electronics, chemicals, pharmaceuticals, biomedical sciences and engineering, which contribute substantially to Singapore's economic growth.

In the early days of Singapore's industrialisation, flatted factories were introduced to ensure optimal use of Singapore's scarce land resource. Today, the pressure to ensure higher productivity for land use has not gone away, especially since Singapore still relies significantly on space-consuming manufacturing industries.

Creating space

Thus, more "out-of-the-box" space solutions are required. One of these is the "ramp-up" factory. These go beyond the flatted factories of yore in offering ground floor-like vehicular access on each floor, achieved through the construction of ramps for direct vehicular access to factories on every floor. Motor vehicle workshops, which take up lots of land, have been successfully transplanted into these "ramp-up" factories in places like Ang Mo Kio.

Intensifying use

Despite intensification of use, it has been estimated in the Concept Plan 2001 that the amount of land required for industry will rise by 6,000 hectares to more than 12,500 · hectares in the long run. The supply of this land will be partly met through reclamation. Between 1991 and 1999, the URA and JTC planned the amalgamation of seven islands through reclamation to form Jurong Island, to house an off-shore petrochemicals hub.

Under the Concept Plan, high-intensity industries will be located close to MRT stations, major roads and bus interchanges to facilitate ease of commuting. More land will be set aside for high-value industries like wafer fabrication and pharmaceuticals.

FOL

"A photograph is made on the spot and at once. You have no right to use tricks or play around with reality. The time element is the key to photography. One must seize the moment before it passes. The fleeting gesture, the evanescent smile."

- Henri Cartier-Bresson,
French photojournalist

08

Island life

Celebrating life on the water's edge

I N Singapore, you are never too far away from the water's edge. Whether it's the sea, a river, or reservoir, it can be reached in a matter of minutes rather than hours, from any point on the island - even by public transport. And, indeed, Singaporeans and visitors alike are constantly lured to the water's edge - for a spot of romantic wining and dining, sports, or simply, for unwinding after a long hard day.

Singapore's waterfronts offer a wide variety of experiences - from the urban (Boat Quay and Esplanade) to the rustic (Changi Creek, Sungei Buloh and Chek Jawa) and recreational (East Coast Park, Kallang River and Pasir Ris Park). From the transitory (boardwalks at MacRitchie Reservoir and Changi Point) to the more sedentary (waterfront housing at Tanjong Rhu, Punggol 21, Pasir Ris, and soon, Sentosa Cove), to the active (water sports centres at Punggol and East Coast).

Expect to get wet

As a result, enjoying life by the water's edge has become a quintessentially Singaporean

LOWE unlimited – Balmy breezes, lapping waves, soft sand underfoot; the stuff of Life On the Water's Edge

Photograph by *Ashleigh Sim*
Streats

Hot boards – Surf's up; beach boys descend on East Coast Park

Photograph by *Ashleigh Sim*
Streats

Primary education – With plans to double Singapore's existing coastline through future reclamation, these kids are getting a good grounding for the future

Photograph by *Ashleigh Sim*
Streats

Spinning, tanning – Multi-tasking on the beach

Photograph by *Ashleigh Sim*
Streats

pastime over the years. In the Concept Plan 2001, the URA enshrined the need to protect and develop this trait by elevating Singapore's "island-ness" as a focus of its future planning efforts.

In collaboration with the Public Utilities Board, access and activities on the water's edge will also be promoted. Already, canoes and brightly-coloured sails make for a postcard-pretty scene at Bedok Reservoir. Non-motorised water activities such as canoeing and sculling are also allowed at the Pandan, MacRitchie and Lower Seletar reservoirs. Already, thanks to collaborative efforts with NParks, popular public amenities like the boardwalk skirting the emerald waters of MacRitchie Reservoir and its look-out tower have been completed. The newly-completed tree-top walkway adds to this experience, offering a unique aerial vantage from where the resident wildlife can be observed in its natural habitat.

Two's company – The sea view is hard to beat for doing what comes naturally

Photograph by *Ashleigh Sim*
Streats

Lagoon life – Last catch at East Coast Lagoon

Photograph by *Ashleigh Sim*
Streats

When Kallang River was cleaned up, new beaches were specially created in collaboration with the ENV, by placing sand on the otherwise muddy bank. Today, the beach is a popular picnic spot where you can enjoy watching wake boarders and their aqua acrobatics, or canoeists gliding by on the calm, clean waters. And so, the Singaporean love affair with life at the water's edge continues.

Whiz wheels – With more of Singapore's 150km-long coastline being opened for recreational uses, more people are heading seawards

Photograph by *Ashleigh Sim*
Streats

Rush City

L IKE New York built inside Central Park - this arresting image of Singapore as a city in a garden was painted by Professor Tommy Koh, who later chaired the Earth Summit in Rio de Janeiro in 1992. Its origins, however, go back 30 years.

It all began when Mr Lee Kuan Yew, Singapore's first Prime Minister, planted a tree in 1963. It seeded a green revolution and the vision of a city in a garden. More than 730,000 trees and 3 million shrubs later, Singapore is closer to that vision. But the pace of greening has only snowballed, thanks to NParks' efforts.

The Concept Plan 2001 provides for almost a doubling of the 2,500 hectares of open green spaces on the island to 4,500 hectares. This is equivalent to 34 more Bishan Parks.

Green, green grass of home
The popular Bishan Park was planned by HDB as a regional park. Sandwiched between Bishan and Ang Mo Kio, it serves their residents, yet acts as a physical buffer, demarcating and identifying them as distinct HDB Towns.

More greenery would not be of use if you can't get to it. And so, the Concept Plan also provides for these green spaces to be more accessible through an extended network of Park Connectors that link parks with town centres, sports centres and homes. For instance, from another regional park - Pasir Ris Park - you will be able to cycle to Bedok Reservoir Park and on to East Coast Park - through a system of Park Connectors.

Making this Park Connector Network a feasible concept requires a multi-agency effort involving the close collaboration of NParks, the Land Transport Authority and the Ministry of the Environment & Water Resources.

Transit stopover – Sungei Buloh is part of the East Asian Australasian Shorebird Site Network, which includes Australia's Kakadu National Park, China's Mai Po and Japan's Yatsu Tidal Flats

Photograph by *Lee Tiah Khee*
Lianhe Zaobao

Life among plants I – Flower beds soak up the sun at Eastwood housing estate (top)

Photograph by *Ho Peng Yew*
Lianhe Zaobao

Life among plants II – China Square. Greening the city has been hardwired in the Singaporean psyche since Mr Lee Kuan Yew kick-started Tree Planting Day in the 1960s (middle)

Photograph by *Jonathan Choo*
The New Paper

Life among plants III – Raffles Hotel garden. Lush greenery is the backdrop of life in this tropical metropolis (bottom)

Photograph by *Edwin Koo*
Streats

Light my way – Family exploring the wonders of Sungei Buloh Wetland Reserve, an ecological gem set in urban Singapore

Photograph by *Lee Tiah Khee*
Lianhe Zaobao

Rustic areas retained

New rustic areas have also been safeguarded.
Unlike the Concept Plan 1991 which proposed
new towns at Pulau Ubin and Lim Chu Kang,
the current Concept Plan 2001 aims to retain
these rustic areas for as long as possible. Areas
such as Sungei China Mangrove at Woodlands
will be integrated within parks so that more
people can enjoy their natural charms.

Meanwhile, the URA and the NParks have
extended Singapore's premier garden - the
Singapore Botanic Gardens. At another historic
green location - Fort Canning Park - the early
history of Singapore has been incorporated
into the experience of the greenery.

Painted sky – Glorious sunsets are just one of the spectacular
nature offerings at Sungei Buloh

Photograph by *Lee Tiah Khee*
Lianhe Zaobao

Dropping in on nature

IT is not difficult to drop in on nature when nature is at your doorstep. Residents of such housing estates as Pasir Ris and Bedok Reservoir know this.

Jogging along the bank of the manmade Bedok Reservoir at dawn, for instance, you'll hear the trill of wild birds mingling incongruously with the distant rumble of heavy traffic along the Bedok Reservoir Road.

Welcome to the nature-hood

At Sungei Api Api, a river that runs through Pasir Ris, mudskippers conference lazily in the ebbing tide among mangrove roots - within sight of towering HDB blocks. This is not coincidental charm, but the result of a conscious undertaking to have a soft, natural-looking edge incorporated in the landscaping works for the river, instead of the usual concrete edge.

Such undertakings were facilitated through URA's chairmanship of the Waterbodies Design Panel comprising members from both public and private sectors to look into the aesthetic treatment of waterbodies in Singapore.

Closer to nature

Increasingly, Singaporeans will be able to enjoy nature at their doorsteps as the URA's Parks and Waterbodies Plan is implemented in collaboration with its partner agencies. In 2004, the URA sponsored a design competition for two link bridges in the Southern Ridges as part of a bigger plan to allow pedestrians to traverse the 9 kilometre chain of hills from Kent Ridge to Mount Faber.

A river runs through it – A soft-banked Sungei Api Api runs through Pasir Ris housing estate

Photograph by *Chew Seng Kim*
The Straits Times

Marsh fellows I - Dragonfly hovers
Photograph by *Lee Tiah Khee*
Lianhe Zaobao

Marsh fellows II - Grey heron takes flight
Photograph by *Lee Tiah Khee*
Lianhe Zaobao

Marsh fellows III - Odd fish out
Photograph by *Lee Tiah Khee*
Lianhe Zaobao

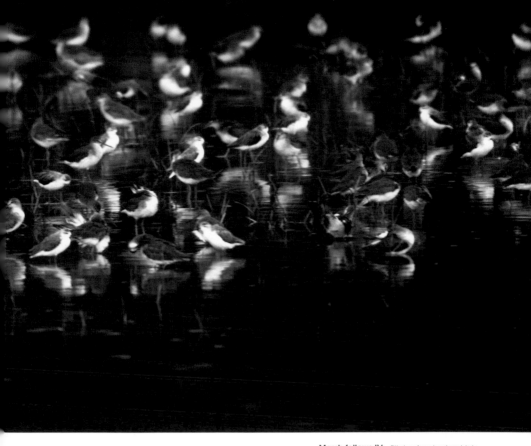

Marsh fellows IV - Pit stop for migratory birds
Photograph by *Lee Tiah Khee*
Lianhe Zaobao

The URA also facilitated the extension of the conserved wetland habitat in Sungei Buloh from 87 to 131 hectares in January, 2002. Renamed the Sungei Buloh Wetland Reserve, it was gazetted as a Nature Reserve. The reserve is home to more than 500 species of tropical flora and fauna and is a "refuelling point" for migratory birds on the East Asian Flyway.

Leafy downtown

At Downtown at Marina Bay, more leafy experiences await. Already the verdant Marina City Park, with its mature trees, emerald lake and fountain attracts strollers and joggers along its shaded paths. The future downtown will be graced by even more parks that offer pedestrians shady green canopies amid the shimmering skyscrapers to be built there.

Ecological gem

THINK "marine life" and Singapore would not figure on the radar screen - not at least before December 2000, when an ecological gem was discovered right under our noses - Chek Jawa.

The discovery

Washed by tidal currents off the eastern end of Pulau Ubin, just off the starboard wings of the train of planes landing at Changi Airport, the discovery astounded even nature buffs. They never imagined such a sanctuary of rich marine life could exist in Singapore waters.

Word of this discovery spread, and soon, Chek Jawa became an outdoor classroom in marine biodiversity. After all, Chek Jawa boasted six ecosystems in one - mangroves, coastal hill forest, sandy ecosystems, rocky shore, seagrass lagoon and coral rubble.

But there was a dilemma: the eastern end of Pulau Ubin was slated for reclamation. This included Chek Jawa. Fresh from the excitement of their discovery, nature lovers had to contend with its loss. The Nature Society of Singapore and Raffles Museum of Biodiversity Research hurriedly organised talks and outings for the public to see Singapore's marine wonder before it was all gone. Letters pleading for the saving of Chek Jawa appeared in the press.

A dilemma

Their pleas did not go unheard. On 19 October, 2001, Minister for National Development Mah Bow Tan personally visited Chek Jawa to see for himself if the place lived up to its rapidly rising reputation. Once there, he understood the basis of those passionate public pleas.

"But we were faced with a dilemma," Mr Mah wrote in the foreward of the book Chek Jawa, Discovering Singapore's Biodiversity, "Land is scarce in Singapore. Reclaiming land allows us to stretch our limited land resources to meet our needs. Could we keep Chek Jawa while still ensuring that our critical land use needs could be met?"

Treasure Island – Chek Jawa's mudflats off Pulau Ubin are a treasure trove of sea life

Photograph by *Stephanie Yeow*
The Straits Times

Win-win, for now

Adopting a balanced and pragmatic approach to land use planning, a URA-led review team issued a measured reprieve that recognised the value of this ecological gem, the passion of nature-loving Singaporeans and the long-term interests of Singapore: Chek Jawa will not be reclaimed for as long as it is not needed for development.

The reprieve came on 21 December 2001, just days before reclamation works were to commence. In his book, Chek Jawa, Chua Ee Kiam wrote: "It was quite unexpected, unprecedented and courageous to defer land reclamation when so much had gone into the preparation of the process. Stunned disbelief was the widespread reaction."

In Chek Jawa, the government demonstrated that public opinion does play a pivotal role in shaping public policy.

Watch your step! – Enthusiastic crowds descending on Chek Jawa's fragile ecosystem caused concern among nature lovers, leading to better visitor management systems being put in place (right)

Photograph by *Stephanie Yeow*
The Straits Times

Skippers' conference – Mudskippers bask and "banter"

Photograph by *Ray Chua*
Lianhe Zaobao

Tidal treasure – Sea anemone at Chek Jawa

Photograph by *Ray Chua*
Lianhe Zaobao

Mermaid's pasture – Large marine mammals like dugongs, which have been found in Pulau Ubin's waters, graze on such underwater greens

Photograph by *Ray Chua*
Lianhe Zaobao

Historic coastline

AS far removed from the bustle of the city as one can be on Singapore Island, Changi has, throughout its history, been associated with the laidback, picnicking and beach-combing ways of generations of Singaporeans. For these memories, there's no place quite like Changi in Singapore.

Today, the development of sailing clubs, holiday chalets, pubs and coffee shops, and a hotel have enhanced Changi's image as a destination for holiday-making on home soil. In its plans for the future of Changi, the URA aims to further enhance this rustic feel while improving the level of public amenities in the area.

Kelong-like boardwalk
One of the URA's initiatives is the construction of a boardwalk skirting the historic coastline of

Baywatch 1976 – Changi Beach has always been a favourite haunt of beachcombers as seen in this photograph from 1976 (left)

Photograph courtesy of *National Archives Singapore*

Walk into the sunset – The Changi Boardwalk, in its scenic setting, has proven a popular haunt for Singaporeans wanting some peace and quiet (below)

Photograph by *Stephanie Yeow*
The Straits Times

Changi. The 1.2km western half of this boardwalk, stretching from Changi Sailing Club to the rocky coast near the Changi Beach Club was completed in September 2003.

With its vantage views and quaint traditional architecture, the boardwalk has become a favourite spot for anglers and sunset strollers. Their promenading pleasure will soon be further enhanced when a 1.5km long park connector along Netheravon Road is completed. This will be connected to the larger 35km loop, linking Changi Beach Park, Pasir Ris Park, Bedok Reservoir Park and East Coast Park.

New ferry terminal

The old ferry terminal at Changi must have been the most modest of Singapore's ingress points, complete with its bumboat terminal, immigration checkpoint, police post and lone diesel pump for the boats. For decades, holiday-makers, army recruits and fish farmers would wait here for the tide to come up, before jumping gingerly from boat to boat to get to their launches for the short trip across the sea to Pulau Ubin or Tekong.

A new ferry terminal is nearing completion. The design preserves sea views and the rustic character of the locale. Its roof will feature a garden with some of the indigenous trees of Changi.

The waiting game – Anglers enjoy the sunset while waiting for a bite

Photograph by *Stephanie Yeow*
The Straits Times

FOL

To consult the rules of composition before making a picture is little like consulting the law of gravitation before going for a walk.

- *Edward Weston*,
American photographer

09

Selling excellence

Celebrated city

Going forth – Those who are knowledgeable of Singapore's attributes are her best ambassadors. URA's initiatives to promote an awareness and appreciation of architecture and urban design excellence aims to raise the bar on this count

Photograph by *Long Kwok Hong*
Lianhe Zaobao

THE Singapore River. Chinatown. the Esplanade - Theatres on the Bay.

Do your own straw poll and ask Singaporeans where their favourite place in Singapore is. Chances are, these three places would crop up as the top three, and in that order too.

How can we be so sure? Well, simply because we asked the same question in the "My City" national photographic competition, launched in conjunction with the Shaping Singapore exhibition. The answer came back loud and clear – to the tune of some 550 photographs of more than 90 places in Singapore.

More than a fifth of the entrants chose the Singapore River – the firm favourite, followed by Chinatown and the Esplanade - Theatres on the Bay. This is not surprising, nor is the inclusion of such popular subjects as The Fullerton Hotel, Bugis Junction and China Square, since these projects have also earned national and international acclaim for their architecture and urban design.

Timely thrust

This enthusiastic response certainly indicates that Singaporeans are not apathetic about the city we live in. Indeed, at the dawn of the new millennium, with Singapore's urban development having reached a tertiary phase, Singaporeans are beginning to celebrate the city we live in – and not a decade too soon. For we have entered an era when global competition for the best brains and business has never been keener; a time when a city's urban profile can play a crucial role in whether such global talents decide to come and contribute, and even sink roots, or pass us by.

Increasingly, what separates successful cities from the "also-rans" in attracting global talent and business lies in their ability to offer the good life, above and beyond sound infrastructure, efficient and transparent administration, cost-effectiveness and proximity to markets. In a word, what distinguishes such successful cities from their competitors is *design*, which can catalyse an upward spiral of growth that would yield tangible material benefits beyond aesthetic endowment.

Reflecting on our city – Each space and piece of architecture that we enjoy in the city has a story to tell about how it came to be. Understanding, for instance, how Chijmes' UNESCO award-winning restoration was achieved only with much engineering ingenuity enhances our enjoyment of it

Photograph by *Ashleigh Sim*
Streats

Design dividends

Cities like London, New York, Manchester, Bilbao, Sydney and Melbourne have reaped tangible economic benefits from investing in the promotion of good design. Interestingly, their experience has also shown that, while good design contributes to the economy, it does not necessarily cost more to build and maintain, nor take longer to construct.

With an exciting city already taking shape, Singapore is poised to benefit from initiatives to promote its urban profile internationally, so as to compete for the cream of global talent and investment on an equal footing. In recent years, the URA has launched other initiatives to promote an awareness and appreciation of architecture and urban design excellence, in collaboration with relevant partners from the public and private sectors. We hope these initiatives will further encourage Singaporeans to appreciate their own city.

City canvas – The best mix of old and new designs makes for a progressive city that remembers its past

Photograph by *Lee Tiah Khee*
Lianhe Zaobao

Competing for the best

DESIGN competitions are one way of obtaining good designs for buildings. Internationally as well as in Singapore, architectural competitions have yielded numerous outstanding designs.

Long history

Singapore has a long history of architectural competitions. From the formative years of the 1960s and 70s came the NTUC Conference Hall, the Science Centre and the PUB Headquarters building.

The Esplanade, Theatres on The Bay and the NTUC Headquarters are two distinctive competition buildings that were recently completed. And soon the National Library, Singapore Management University and Circle Line MRT stations – all derived from architectural competitions–– will be completed.

This tradition is set to continue. In November 2003, the URA announced the 10 winning designs in the 10 Public Spaces Design Ideas Competition, which was held in conjunction the "Our City Centre" exhibition. The contest sought innovative, people-friendly public space designs from the public.

Also in November 2003, the URA launched the Southern Ridges Bridges Design Competition,

in which five schemes were eventually given Merit Awards. Of these, two have been picked to be built.

A public test

However, the competition project that has generated the biggest buzz of late is The Pinnacle@Duxton, a sell-out inner city public housing scheme.

The competition, launched in August 2001, sought fresh, new and innovative solutions for very high-rise, high-density public housing. To cast the net as wide as possible, the international architectural fraternity was invited to participate. A distinguished international panel of judges was appointed, which included the Pritzker Prize laureate Professor Fumihiko Maki and Professor Moshe Safdie, whose seminal Habitat concept for utopian urban living remains a lasting 20th century icon.

The competition, a first for public housing in Singapore, attracted 202 entries from the world over. In the end, the design called "Sky houses, flying green" by a young Singapore architectural practice, Arc Studio, was declared the winner in April 2002.

Imagine – Some of the 4,953 applicants coveting a unit in the 1,848-apartment development

Photograph by *Alan Lim*
The Straits Times

The Pinnacle@Duxton

The Peak

Sell-out skyscraper – The international architectural competition to find a design for Singapore's first 50-storey public housing scheme yielded a successful design that fired the imagination of the buying public

Photograph by *Alan Lim*
The Straits Times

Overwhelming response

When Phase One of the 50-storey, 1,848-unit project was launched in May 2004, it attracted an overwhelming response. Many of those who applied for a unit cited location and the award-winning design as principal reasons for their interest. For a project whose target audience is the heartland Singaporean, this is truly a ringing endorsement of the success of the competition system in producing good architectural designs.

Getting design under your skin

ONE of the best ways to promote good architecture and urban design is to showcase good examples of it in exhibitions, invite the designers to come and give public talks, and, for the record, put it all down in a book that people can read, keep, and share, long after the exhibition and talks are over.

Reaching out

It is therefore no wonder that the URA, in furthering its agenda of promoting an awareness and appreciation of architecture and urban design excellence, has been organising exhibitions and talks and publishing books:

○ November 1999: "Home Work Play", a book on the URA's planning and urban design efforts and its vision for Singapore was published. It was written by journalist Sumiko Tan.

○ September 2000: Exhibition on "A Unique City in the Making", featuring the URA's Landmark & Gateway Plan was opened.

○ April 2001: Joint URA-STB exhibition on "Making Orchard Road more happening!" opened.

○ July 2002: URA launched the Parks and Waterbodies Plan and Identity Plan as innovative frameworks to guide the review of Master Plan 2003. These plans aim to retain and enhance the areas of nature, greenery and identity in Singapore.

○ June 2003: Exhibition on "Our City Centre – A great place to live, work and play", illustrating the Public Space & Urban Waterfront Master Plan, Downtown at Marina Bay, City Living at Pearl's Hill, and Bras Basah.Bugis plan was opened.

○ June 2003: The Design Ideas Competition for 10 Public Spaces was launched.

○ June 2003: Unveiled plans for a distinctive Downtown at Marina Bay, a seamless extension of the CBD.

○ August 2003: Exhibition of the recent works Pritzker Prize laureate Fumihiko Maki entitled: "Modernity and the Construction of Scenery" opened.

○ October 2003: Annual Architectural Heritage Awards ceremony and exhibition held.

○ March 2004: Inaugural exhibition: "20 under 45: A selection of works by under-45, Singapore-registered Architects" was launched. This was a collaboration with the Board of Architects, National University of Singapore, Real Estate Developers Association of Singapore and Singapore Institute of Architects. A public roundtable discussion and talks by 15 of the featured architects were organised in conjunction

Exposed II – Another icon rises? The Norman Foster-designed Supreme Court Building being erected behind Singapore's newest urban icon, The Esplanade. Being open to such world-renowned talent is another route to a prominent international profile (top)

Exposed III – Assyafaah Mosque. Inhabiting such award-winning designs subconsciously instils a keener awareness and appreciation of good design (right)

Photographs by *Ho Peng Yew*
Lianhe Zaobao

Exposed I - Church of St Mary of the Angels. World-class architecture by local design talents have been given local and international platforms through such vehicles as the "20 under 45" exhibition and catalogue and the Venice Biennale

Photograph by *Ng Sor Luan*
Streats

with the exhibition. The catalogue was on the bestseller list of Kinokuniya bookstore.

o August 2004: Talk by avant garde Japanese architect Toyo Ito.

o October 2004: Annual Architectural Heritage Awards ceremony and exhibition was held.

o December 2004:
"Shaping Singapore: Achievements (1974 – 2004) & Aspirations (2004 – 2034)", a photojournalistic portrayal of the story of Singapore's urban development over the past 30 years, with a virtual glimpse of the next 30 years was launched. The exhibition is a collaboration with Singapore Press Holdings.

o December 2004:
"My City" photographic competition was held in conjunction with the Shaping Singapore exhibition. The 18 prize winners were selected by a URA- SPH panel and reproduced in a charity calendar.

o December 2004: The URA Gallery was reopened as the revamped "City Gallery",

a popular visitor centre for students and the general public showing how creative planning can overcome Singapore's physical constraints to meet her development needs.

Watch this space

In addition to more exhibitions, talks and publications, new mechanisms for the promotion of an appreciation of architecture and urban design, such as the co-funding of projects like publications, events, multimedia productions, research studies and competitions will follow.

Concurrently, the URA is working towards a greater alignment of thrusts to promote quality architecture and urban design with other interested parties to leverage of the collective synergy of this emerging movement in Singapore.

239

What the future holds

S INGAPORE has come a long way since Stamford Raffles set foot here in 1819. No doubt, the city will continue evolving, preserving the best of its heritage, while embracing new architecture and urban design to serve the needs of future Singaporeans.

To these future citizens of our city, this collection of photographs will be a precious portrait of Singapore, circa 2004. It constitutes a testament of 30 years of city building since the founding of the URA, through the synergistic collaboration of both the private and public sectors - a process that continues apace to achieve an even better future.

The medium of photojournalism used in this exhibition is a deliberate choice. For photojournalism is, as succinctly defined by Mr Edwin Koo, one of the young photojournalists whose works are featured here: "the mastery of truth - telling stories with pictures, rather than words." What you see here is the true face of the Singapore we have built collectively.

The moment these photographs were snapped, however, they have passed into the past - our collective past. Hopefully, down the road, these images will remind us of our connectedness to each other as fellow citizens. And imbue in us a sense of belonging to Singapore, for we share a common root in the life and times of our forefathers who built this city. Passed into the hands of future generations of Singapore, this heritage will be their due inheritance.

Reason to smile – Poised to inherit and build upon this city, these scions of Singapore have reason to rejoice

Photograph by *Spencer Chung Kun Soon*
Lianhe Zaobao

241

Appendix 1

Lt Jackson Plan, 1822 –
Following his historic founding
of Singapore in 1819, Stamford
Raffles left the island and
returned three years later
to find, to his dismay, that
development had proceeded
in a haphazard way. He
directed Lieutenant Philip
Jackson, the engineer and
land surveyor in charge of
overseeing the island's
development, to draw up
Singapore's first development
plan in 1822. This plan
enshrined Raffles' directive for
the various ethnic groups to be
housed in separate quarters
and set out the arterial road
structure which remains till
today.

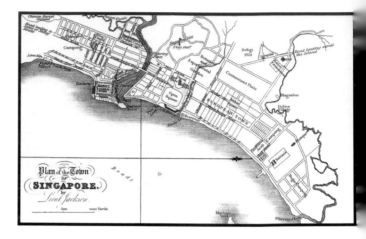

Appendix 2

Master Plan 1958 – This was
Singapore's first Statutory
Master Plan drawn up by the
British colonial government in
response to the settlement's
crying need for forward
planning to alleviate the
acute housing shortage,
chronic congestion in the city
centre and to guide land use
through zoning density and
plot ratio controls. The Plan
featured a "green belt" to
arrest the growth of the city
centre, and the development
of outlying new towns and
key villages as centres of
agricultural development.

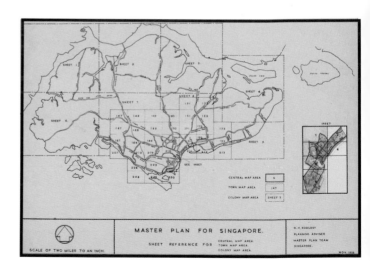

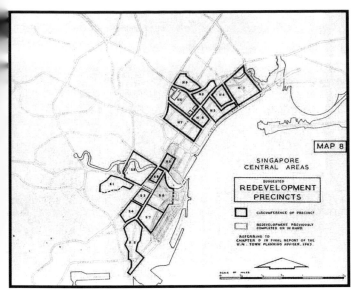

Appendix 3:

Lorange Plan, 1962 – Following self-rule in 1959, the newly-elected government of Singapore inherited a city whose urban planning had been neglected for about 120 years. In 1962, the government invited the United Nations town planning advisor, Professor Erik Lorange, to propose a long-term planning proposal for Singapore. The Lorange Plan proposed that the city be divided into precincts that could be developed independently. Two high-rise, high-density projects, at Crawford and Outram, were completed in the late 1970s according to this plan.

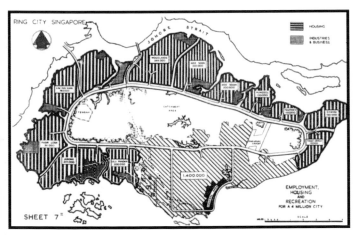

Appendix 4:

Koenigsberger Plan, 1963 – The second United Nations planning team under Professor Otto Koenigsberger arrived in 1963 and proposed an integrated approach to housing, urban renewal, industrial development and transportation. The Koenigsberger Plan catered to a population of 4 million and proposed a "ring city" concept wherein a necklace of new towns, connected by a road network, surrounds a central water catchment area. In his scheme, no one would live more than 1.6km from the sea or an open space.

Appendix 5:

Concept Plan 1971 – This plan was proposed by the State and City Planning Project, carried out with United Nations' help between 1967 and 1971. The Master Plan 1958 was found to be ineffective in addressing Singapore's rapid economic expansion and massive housing programmes of the 1960s. As a result, the Concept Plan 1971, a "ring concept plan", was adopted after considering previous planning proposals, including the Koenigsberger Plan. New high-density satellite towns would surround the central catchment area, interspersed with lower density housing areas among green wedges of parks and open spaces. Industry was catered for – in Jurong. And a new airport – in Changi – was also proposed.

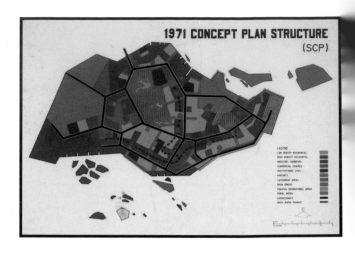

Appendix 6:

Central Area Structure Plan, 1985 – In 1983, the URA completed an urban design plan for the Central Area that would guide the orderly transformation of the city skyline and seamlessly stitch its historical, architectural and cultural assets into the urban fabric. This plan was published in 1985 as the Central Area Structure Plan.

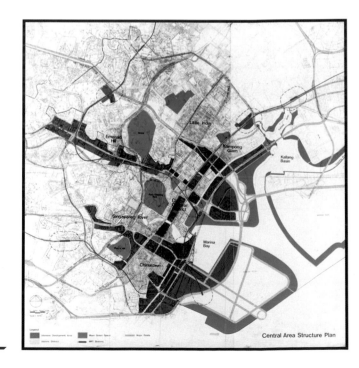

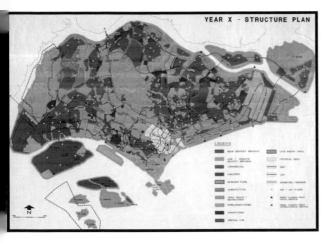

YEAR X - STRUCTURE PLAN

Appendix 7:

Concept Plan 1991 – By 1989, most of the proposals contained in the Concept Plan 1971 had already been achieved – new towns, expressways, the MRT system, Jurong industrial estate, Changi Airport, and the development of the Central Area was almost complete. The time had come to chart the next lap of Singapore's development – as "a tropical city of excellence" – for a population of 4 million. To facilitate the realisation of its proposals, the Concept Plan 1991 was translated into 55 Development Guide Plans, Detailed Plans for Implementation and Urban Design Plans.

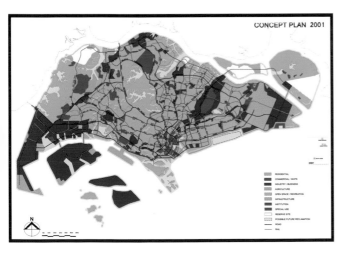

CONCEPT PLAN 2001

Appendix 8:

Concept Plan 2001 – This current Plan maps the vision for Singapore's development in the next 40 to 50 years. It is based on a population scenario of 5.5 million and addresses the challenges of meeting the demands of economic and population growth against the scarcity of land. This Plan makes key proposals for housing, recreation, business and infrastructure building, while reinforcing identity so as to make Singapore a dynamic, distinctive and delightful city of the 21st century.

Appendix 9:

Parks & Waterbodies and Identity Plan, 2002 – This Plan helps to ensure the enhancement of Singapore's green spaces, waterbodies and living environment. Among other things, the Plan proposes the development of new parks, 120km of park connectors, greener streetscapes, and the opening up of more waterfront features. The Plan also recognises the need to make Singapore a distinctive city by retaining and enhancing the unique aspects of the island's built heritage. The retention and development of places and uses were proposed under four headings – Old World Charm, Urban Villages, Southern Ridges and Hillside Villages, and Rustic Coast.

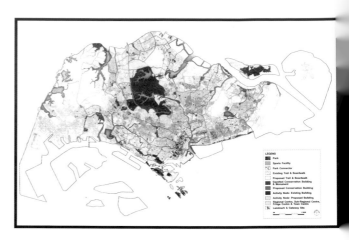

Appendix 10:

Master Plan 2003 – This current edition of the Statutory Master Plan, gazetted on 10 December 2003, is Singapore's blueprint for physical development over the next 10 to 15 years. The key focus is to build and improve on the quality of our living environment, provide greater flexibility for businesses and retain the identity of unique places. It incorporates the proposals for the 55 Planning Areas, the Parks and Waterbodies Plan and the Identity Plan in terms of land use and development density for the whole island.

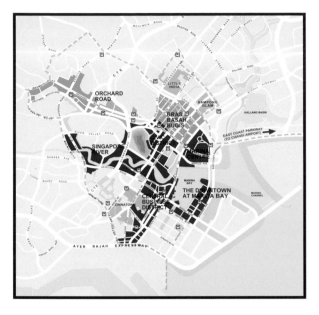

Appendix 11:

District Character Plan for Central Area, 2003 – This Plan maps the distinct identities of various districts of the Central Area so as to project it as a great place to live, work and play in. It highlights the dynamic, distinctive and delightful aspects of these city quarters – the Downtown, Civic District, Bras Basah.Bugis, Singapore River and Orchard Road – to enhance the enjoyment of these spaces and places, and to ensure that their future development reinforces these characteristics.

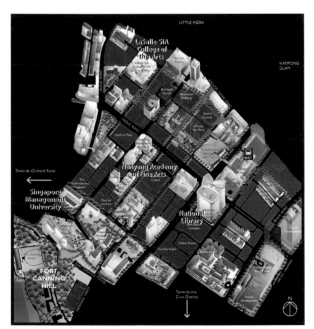

Appendix 12:

Bras Basah.Bugis axonometric, 2003 – This bird's eye rendering of the Bras Basah.Bugis district encapsulates the URA's vision of the district's potential to be an arts, culture, learning and entertainment hub. The distinctive architecture and setting of the various educational campuses, such as the Singapore Management University, Nanyang Academy of Fine Arts, and LaSalle-SIA College of the Arts, are depicted in 3D. The drawing also illustrates how the proximity of local landmarks, such as Bugis Village, Albert Mall, and Fort Canning Park complement the new uses and reinforce the buzz of the area.

Chew Seng Kim, 48, is a Straits Times stalwart, with 20 years experience as a photojournalist under his belt. A former Navy man who loves being on the move, the job of a photojournalist suited him to a 'T' - especially since photography is his love. After seven years with the Navy, Seng Kim honed his craft as a freelance photographer for five years, before joining The Straits Times. Having been on both sides of the photography - photojournalism divide, Seng Kim simply defines the difference between the two as "in photojournalism, you have no time to say 'cheese'. Our job is to capture an event or moment accurately and informatively".

Jonathan Choo, 47, is a photojournalist with The New Paper who has been shooting photographs for 30 years. Although he names no favourite photographer, his favourite subjects for photography are sports and fashion. Outside of photography, his interests include mountain biking and nature, which explains why his favourite place in Singapore is the Bukit Timah Nature Reserve. Of his enduring interest in his craft, Jonathan would only say that he keeps clicking simply because his passion for photography has never faded.

Spencer Chung Kun Soon, 35, was 18 when he first touched a camera. He can't recall the circumstances of that milestone event, but chances are, he was in the company of "lots of colourful people", and beer - the two requisites Spencer says will transform any location to his favourite spot in Singapore. That is, aside from the Lianhe Zaobao photojournalist's home, where he indulges in his favourite activities of sleep and playing his X-Box. Spencer debunks the hero-worship of famous photographers. Anyone who can shoot with a compact camera can produce a great shot, he said.

Joyce Fang, 32, graduated in business from the University of Oklahoma but a temp stint at a bank confirmed it for her that she didn't want to pursue a career in business. Although business is perceived as being a stable profession, her interests in the arts and photography held sway. Leaving the world of dollars and cents, Joyce first joined a local theatre company as a props manager and then a commercial photography studio, for a year. In 1998, she joined The Straits Times.

Ho Peng Yew, 28, is a chip off the old block as far as photography is concerned. Under his father's tutelage, he never forgot to bring along a compact camera each time he went on a school excursion. During his National Service he was an army photographer, an experience, he says, that has taught him to face challenges squarely. Today, "the challenge" continues to keep this Nanyang Polytechnic graduate honing his craft to reach his self-set standards. Not surprisingly, the Lianhe Zaobao photojournalist is his own favourite photographer. Marine aquaria, badminton and mini remote controlled cars are Peng Yew's other passions.

Simon Ker, 46, started on photography 25 years ago as a hobby. The New Paper photographer's favourite subjects are children, because they are "cute" and are a "fun" subject. Aside from photography, Simon's other passions include collecting automatic watches and antique radios.

Edwin Koo, 26, graduated in mass communications from the Nanyang Technological University and joined Streats. Despite a late brush with photography (he first touched an SLR camera only at university) Edwin won the local Happy Wrinkles photo competition and took second place in the international ClickArt 2003 World Photojournalist Meet (Behind the Scenes category). He also participated in the World Press Photo Young Photographer's Forum in Hanoi, 2004. John Stanmeyer is a major influence because "he made me look hard at the power of truth and what photojournalism can do to bring about that truth". "Truth" and "social issues" as his favourite subjects.

Lee Tiah Khee, 39, is a 1992 Young Artist Award winner who took up photography when he joined his school club at 14 on the encouragement of his father. Though he has no formal training, the Chief Photographer at Lianhe Zaobao has won many awards and participated in numerous exhibitions locally, as well as in Hong Kong and China. He attributes his success to passion and the inspiration of his favourite photographer, Frans Lanting. Tiah Khee's favourite places are the beach and nature reserves where he seeks peace and indulgence in shooting his favourite subjects - nature and landscapes.

Alan Lim, 31 studied photography at the Art Institute of Fort Lauderdale in Florida, graduating in 1995 with an associate degree of science in photography. Returning to Singapore, he decided to seek a faster paced environment and Alan found that photojournalism offered just such a challenge. In 1997 he joined The Straits Times photo desk where he has remained since.

Long Kwok Hong, 29, is a Lianhe Zaobao photojournalist who took up photography at school as a extra curricular activity when he was 13. He never imagined that it would be his professional calling. Till today, Kwok Hong feeds on curiosity as the driving force that keeps him interested in his craft. His favourite subjects are people and the environment. Despite the debate about the differences between photography and photojournalism, Kwok Hong feels that they have the same objective - to communicate.

Mohd Ishak Samon, 43, is a veteran with The New Paper whose brush with photography began as a hobby when he was in his 20s. The self-taught photojournalist worked with the now-defunct Singapore Monitor newspaper and Singapore Mass Rapid Transit before joining Singapore Press Holdings. In his 14 years with SPH, Ishak has won four SPH annual awards, for Feature Picture of the Year 2004, Special Award for Excellence 2004, News Picture of the Year 2000, and News Picture of the Year 1998. He is also a Gold Award winner for "Best in digital photography - News" at the international IFRA Publish Asia competition 2002. The car and mountain biking enthusiast loves sports and people photography and Little India for its non-stop bustle.

Ng Sor Luan, 26, a communication studies graduate, took to photography after her first class in photojournalism in 1999 at the Nanyang Technological University. Sor Luan has taken part in local and international competitions such as 759 (2001), Objectifs' "Shooting Home" (2002) and Objectifs' "Shooting Home" II (2003). The Streats photojournalist has also taken part in international exhibitions such as the World Press Photos SEA Jakarta Workshop (2002). A nature buff, Sor Luan dives and considers travel and meeting people as major influences in her work, reminding her to keep an open mind to all kinds of possibilities. Henri Cartier Bresson is her favourite photographer.

Casey Seyu Tzyy Wei, 29, got started on photography the day she rummaged her father's cupboard and discovered a camera. She was then in Primary Three. Her colleagues at Lianhe Zaobao described her as having the steadiest pair of hands on the team - hence her assignment to shoot aerial photographs from a helicopter for Shaping Singapore. In 2004, Casey participated in the Breastfeeding Exposed! exhibition and was a consolation prize winner in the Great Eastern "Life Is Great" photo competition. People are her favourite subject in photography. Her home is her favourite place in Singapore, "because my family and loved ones are there with me".

Ashleigh Sim, 28, is a graduate of the University of Canberra, where she first picked up a camera to document the vicissitudes her life as a foreign student in Australia. Shooting for Shaping Singapore, the blader and beach-lover found herself mixing work with pleasure since she was asked to shoot for the "Island Life" folio, featuring East Coast Park, her favourite place in Singapore. What's more, the Streats photographer loves landscape photography. Ashleigh constantly reminds herself not to expect everyone to appreciate her work. This she learned from her photography lecturer whom she describes as "a man who is passionate about photography and open to ideas", but who hates Ansel Adams "because he is boring".

Terence Tan, 27, knew that he wanted to be a photographer, and not work in IT or engineering like his brothers, after his first foray into photography in an 'O' Level art project in 1993. So he enrolled at Temasek Polytechnic's Visual Communications course, and, by the time he graduated in 1997, already had more than a year's experience in photojournalism as a temp with The Straits Times. His deep interest in his craft didn't prevent him from dabbling in other part-time pursuits "to experience life beyond photography". Before his NS, Terence had already clocked time as a waiter, KFC driver, odd-job labourer and Borders bookseller. He resumed his photojournalistic career with The Straits Times in 1996 after his NS and has been there since.

Dennis Thong Kah Hoong, 33, believes that the photographer's art centres around the ability of the photographer to see the world through his creative eye. He got started on photography when he first glimpsed at the world through the viewfinder of a camera. It changed his thoughts and perspectives of the world. The Lianhe Zaobao photojournalist gets the highest motivation when others express their appreciation of his photography. Dennis' other interests include swimming and scuba diving.

Tukiman Warji, 43, is a self taught photographer who came into his craft "by chance" in 1988. Though the Berita Harian photojournalist may not have attended formal photojournalism classes, he upholds the works of legendary war photographer Robert Capa (whose career ended abruptly in 1954 when he stepped on a landmine in Indochina) and retired Straits Times photographer George Gascon as yardsticks to study and measure his own work against. Asked how he keeps himself interested in his craft, Tukiman simply replies: "To feed my family and because I'm bad in drawing".

Wang Hui Fen, 32, was trained as a graphic designer at the London College of Printing in Graphics and Media Design. Now a Straits Times photojournalist, Hui Fen graduated in 1996 and worked as a graphic designer in an advertising company for three years before she left to pursue her passion for photography. Hui Fen defines photojournalism as "photography for reportage" and, as such, is a genre of photography, which is the generic or umbrella term.

Stephanie Yeow, 33, has been with The Straits Times since 1995. She enrolled in the architecture course at the National University of Singapore but finished only half of the course before pursuing photography. She has not looked back. Starting out with a commercial photo studio, she decided after nine months that lugging heavy studio equipment on location shoots was not how she wanted to spend her working life. She then joined The Straits Times and has been there since.

Acronyms

CAP	-	Conservation Advisory Panel
CAPAM	-	Commonwealth Association for Public Administration and Management
CBD	-	Central Business District
CIS	-	Customer Information System
DBS	-	Development Bank of Singapore
DC	-	Development Control
DGP	-	Development Guide Plans
DTMB	-	Downtown at Marina Bay
ECP	-	East Coast Parkway
EDA	-	Electronic Development Application
ENV	-	Ministry of the Environment and Water Resources
FIABCI	-	International Real Estate Federation
GLS	-	Government Land Sales programme
HDB	-	Housing and Development Board
JTC	-	Jurong Town Corporation
LTA	-	Land Transport Authority
MICA	-	Ministry of Information, Communications and the Arts
MOE	-	Ministry of Education
NAS	-	National Archives of Singapore
NParks	-	National Parks Board
OUB	-	Overseas Union Bank
POWER	-	Public Officers Working to Eliminate Red Tape
PUB	-	Public Utilities Board
SCP	-	State and City Project team
SIA	-	Singapore Institute of Architects
SMU	-	Singapore Management University
STB	-	Singapore Tourism Board
UN	-	United Nations
UOB	-	United Overseas Bank
URA	-	Urban Redevelopment Authority
URD	-	Urban Renewal Department

The Urban Redevelopment Authority wishes to acknowledge the close collaboration of Singapore Press Holdings in making Shaping Singapore: Aspirations (1974 - 2004) & Aspirations (2004 - 2034) a success.

In particular, we wish to thank Mr Lim Jim Koon, Chief Editor of Lianhe Zaobao, Mr Patrick Daniel, Managing Editor of SPH's English and Malay Newspaper Division and Mr David Tay, Chief Executive Officer, SPH Magazines, as well as the editors and photojournalists of Lianhe Zaobao, The Straits Times, The New Paper, Streats and Berita Harian for their sterling contributions:

Mr Paul Jansen, Editor, Streats
Mr Ivan Fernandez, Editor, The New Paper
Mr Guntor Sadali, Editor, Berita Harian
Ms Angelina Choy, Art & Picture Editor, The Straits Times

Lianhe Zaobao photojournalists:
Mr Lee Tiah Khee, Chief Photographer
Mr Spencer Chung Kun Soon
Mr Ho Peng Yew
Mr Long Kwok Hong
Ms Casey Seyu Tzyy Wei
Mr Dennis Thong Kah Hoong

The Straits Times' photojournalists:
Mr Chew Seng Kim
Ms Joyce Fang
Mr Alan Lim
Mr Terence Tan
Ms Wang Hui Fen
Ms Stephanie Yeow

The New Paper's photojournalists:
Mr Simon Ker
Mr Mohd Ishak
Mr Jonathan Choo

Streats' photojournalists:
Mr Edwin Koo
Ms Ng Sor Luan
Ms Ashleigh Sim

Berita Harian's photojournalist:
Mr Tukiman Warji

Special thanks for additional photography:
Mr Ray Chua

On behalf of the URA and SPH:

THANK YOU

For assistance in providing access to buildings for photography or providing images for the Shaping Singapore exhibition:

Asia Insurance Company Ltd ■ The Capitaland Commercial Management Pte Ltd ■ CHIJMES Investment Pte Ltd ■ Church of St Mary of the Angels ■ City Developments Ltd ■ Dlab and WOW Architects ■ Far East Organisation ■ Forum Architects ■ HongKong Land Ltd ■ Housing & Development Board ■ JTC Corporation ■ Keppel Land Ltd ■ Lasalle Foundation Ltd ■ Mapletree Investments Pte Ltd ■ Maplewoods Condominium ■ Marina Mandarin Singapore ■ Marina Properties Pte Ltd ■ Ministry of Defence ■ Prototype71 Design Pte Ltd ■ Raffles Hotel ■ RSP Architects Planners & Engineers Pte Ltd ■ Savu Investment Ltd ■ SCDA Architects ■ Sentosa Leisure Group & Sentosa Cove ■ Singapore Cricket Club ■ Singapore Land Authority ■ Singapore Recreation Club ■ Taher Aamer Design Studio ■ The Arcadia ■ The Arts House at the Old Parliament ■ The Esplanade Company Ltd ■ The Fullerton Singapore ■ The Gateway Land Ltd ■ Toy Factory Theatre Ensemble ■ United Overseas Bank ■ WOHA Architects Pte Ltd

On behalf of the URA:

THANK YOU

The URA's service partners who have collaborated over the last 30 years to make Singapore a great city to live, work and play:

Agency for Science, Technology and Research ■ Agri-Food & Veterinary Authority of Singapore ■ Association of Consulting Engineers, Singapore ■ Board of Architects ■ Building & Construction Authority ■ Civil Aviation Authority of Singapore ■ Defence Science & Technology Agency ■ Economic Development Board ■ Energy Market Authority ■ Health Promotion Board ■ Health Sciences Authority ■ Hotel Licensing Board ■ Housing And Development Board ■ International Enterprise Singapore ■ Infocomm Development Authority of Singapore ■ Inland Revenue Authority of Singapore ■ Institute Of Technical Education ■ JTC Corporation ■ Land Transport Authority ■ Majlis Ugama Islam Singapura ■ Maritime and Port Authority ■ Media Development Authority ■ Ministry of Community Development, Youth and Sports ■ Ministry of Defence ■ Ministry of Education ■ Ministry of Finance ■ Ministry of Foreign Affairs ■ Ministry of Health ■ Ministry of Home Affairs ■ Ministry of Information, Communications and the Arts ■ Ministry of Law ■ Ministry of Manpower ■ Ministry of National Development ■ Ministry of the Environment and Water Resources ■ Ministry of Trade and Industry ■ Ministry of Transport ■ Monetary Authority of Singapore ■ National Arts Council ■ National Council of Social Service ■ National Environment Agency ■ National Heritage Board ■ National Library Board ■ National Parks Board ■ National University of Singapore ■ Nature Society (Singapore) ■ People's Association Preservation of Monuments Board ■ Prime Minister's Office ■ Public Utilities Board ■ Real Estate Developers' Association of Singapore ■ Sentosa Development Corporation ■ Singapore Civil Defence Force ■ Singapore Environmental Council ■ Singapore Heritage Society ■ Singapore Institute of Architects ■ Singapore Institute of Landscape Architects ■ Singapore Institute of Planners ■ Singapore Land Authority ■ Singapore Management University ■ Singapore Police Force ■ Singapore Sports Council ■ Singapore Sports School ■ Singapore Tourism Board ■ Spring Singapore ■ Architectural Design Panel ■ Supervisory Design Panel ■ Waterbodies Design Panel ■ Design Advisory Committee ■ Design Guidelines Waiver Committee ■ Conservation Advisory Panel ■ Design Advisory Panel